ROYAL COURT

Royal Court Theatre presents

WIG OUT!

by **Tarell Alvin McCraney**

First performance at the Royal Court Jerwood Theatre Downstairs,
Sloane Square, London, on 21 November 2008.

Wig Out! was produced by the Vineyard Theater, New York,
Douglas Aibel, Artistic Director, September 2008.

Wig Out! was developed, in part, with the assistance of
the Sundance Institute Theatre Program.

WIG OUT!

by **Tarell Alvin McCraney**

Cast in order of appearance
Fay **Holly Quin-Ankrah**
Fate **Kate Gillespie**
Faith **Jessika Williams** *
Wilson / Nina **Nathan Stewart-Jarrett**
Eric **Alex Lanipekun**
Rey-Rey **Kevin Harvey**
Loki **Drew Caiden**
Lucian **Danny Sapani**
Venus **Craig Stein**
Deity **Leon Lopez**
Serena **Billy Carter**

Director **Dominic Cooke**
Set & Costume Designer **Ultz**
Lighting Designer **Chahine Yavroyan**
Sound Designer **Ian Dickinson**
Choreographer **Manwe**
Music Director **Alex Silverman**
Casting Director **Amy Ball**
Assistant Director **Natalie Ibu**
Assistant Set Designer **Mark Simmonds**
Production Manager **Paul Handley**
Stage Manager **Nafeesah Butt**
Deputy Stage Manager **Vicki Liles**
Assistant Stage Manager **Bryony Drury**
Costume Supervisor **Iona Kenrick**
Hair & Makeup Supervisor **Kerrie-Ann Murphy**
Hair & Makeup Assistant **Cally Bone**
Stylist Intern **Ben Mariah**
Dialect Coach **Penny Dyer**
Stage Management Work Placement **Katie Christ**
Set Built by **Miraculous Engineering**

* Jessika Williams is appearing with the support of UK Equity.

The Royal Court and Stage Management wish to thank the following for
their help with this production: Mr James Bellringer (FRCS), Dennis L. Carney,
Tariano "Celeste" Christie, Zowie Davy, The Event Hire Company,
Specsavers Victoria.

THE COMPANY

TARELL ALVIN McCRANEY (Writer)

THEATRE INCLUDES: The Brothers Size (Studio Theater, Washington/The Public Theater, NY/The Abbey, Dublin with Foundry/ The McCarter Theater, Princeton/Young Vic with ATC); In The Red and Brown Water (Young Vic/Alliance, Atlanta); Marcus or The Secret of Sweet (Alliance, Atlanta); The Breach (Seattle Rep/ Southern Rep); Without/Sin, Run Mourner Run (Yale Cabaret); A Taurian Tale (52nd Street Project); Promise Not To Tell (New World School of The Arts Playwrights Festival).

AWARDS INCLUDE: 2007 Kendala Award for In The Red and Brown Water; 2007 Paula Vogel Playwriting Award; 2007 Whiting Writing Award.

Tarell is the current International Writer in Residence for the RSC, the Hodder Fellow at the Lewis Center for the Arts, Princeton University and holds a seven-year residency at New Dramatists, New York.

DREW CAIDEN (Loki)

THEATRE INCLUDES: Strawberry Daiquiri (US Tour); An Enemy of the People (National); The White Devil, The Merry Wives of Windsor, Macbeth, As You Like It (Oregon Shakespeare Festival); Holiday Memories (Oregon Cabaret).

TELEVISION INCLUDES: MadTV, Rescue 911, Not Like Us.

BILLY CARTER (Serena)

FOR THE ROYAL COURT: Bruises.

THEATRE INCLUDES: The Revenger's Tragedy (National); I'll Be The Devil (RSC/Tricycle); A Moon for the Misbegotten (Old Vic/Broadway); Assassins (Sheffield Crucible); Translations (National & Tour); Macbeth (Almeida); Sergeant Musgrave's Dance, Comedians (Oxford Stage Co.); Eastward Ho!, The Roman Actor, The Island Princess, The Malcontent (RSC/West End); Aristocrats (Chichester); Macbeth (West End); Dealer's Choice (West Yorkshire Playhouse); My Boy Jack (Hampstead); Kes (York Theatre Royal); The Soldier's Song (Stratford East).

TELEVISION INCLUDES: Primeval, Holby City, Fair City, I Fought the Law, M.I.T, The Gist, Up Late with Sean Hughes, The Fitz, Common as Muck, Soldier Soldier, Holding the Baby, Beautiful Day

FILM INCLUDES: Festival, Up on the Roof, Jesus Christ Superstar.

RADIO INCLUDES: Rush

DOMINIC COOKE (Director)

FOR THE ROYAL COURT: Now or Later, War & Peace/Fear & Misery, Rhinoceros, The Pain and the Itch, Other People, Fireface, Spinning into Butter, Redundant, Fucking Games, Plasticine, The People Are Friendly, This is a Chair, Identical Twins.

OTHER THEATRE INCLUDES: Pericles, The Winter's Tale, The Crucible, Postcards from America, Noughts & Crosses, As You Like It, Macbeth, Cymbeline, The Malcontent (RSC); By the Bog of Cats (Wyndham's); The Eccentricities of a Nightingale (Gate, Dublin); Arabian Nights (Young Vic/UK & world tours/New Victory Theatre, New York); The Weavers, Hunting Scenes from Lower Bavaria (Gate); The Bullet (Donmar); Afore Night Come, Entertaining Mr Sloane (Clwyd); The Importance of Being Earnest (Atlantic Theatre Festival, Canada); Caravan (National Theatre of Norway); My Mother Said I Never Should (Oxford Stage Co./Young Vic); Kiss of the Spider Woman (Bolton Octagon); Of Mice and Men (Nottingham Playhouse); Autogeddon (Assembly Rooms).

OPERA INCLUDES: The Magic Flute (WNO); I Capuleti e i Montecchi, La Bohème (Grange Park Opera).

AWARDS INCLUDE: Laurence Olivier Awards for Best Director and Best Revival for The Crucible; TMA Award for Arabian Nights; Fringe First Award for Autogeddon.

Associate director of the Royal Court 1999–2002, associate director of the RSC 2002–2006, assistant director RSC 1992–1993.

Dominic is Artistic Director of the Royal Court.

IAN DICKINSON (Sound)

FOR THE ROYAL COURT: Now or Later, Gone Too Far! The Family Plays, Rhinoceros, My Child, The Eleventh Capital, The Seagull (& Broadway), Krapp's Last Tape, Piano/Forte, Rock 'n' Roll (& Duke of York's/Broadway), Motortown, Rainbow Kiss, The Winterling, Alice Trilogy, Fewer Emergencies, Way to Heaven, The Woman Before, Stoning Mary (& Drum Theatre, Plymouth), Breathing Corpses, Wild East, Dumb Show, Shining City (& Gate, Dublin), Lucky Dog, Blest Be the Tie (with Talawa), Ladybird, Notes on Falling Leaves, Loyal Women, The Sugar Syndrome, Blood, Playing the Victim (with Told By an Idiot), Fallout, Flesh Wound, Hitchcock Blonde (& Lyric), Black Milk, Crazyblackmuthafuckin'self, Caryl Churchill Shorts, Push Up, Fucking Games, Herons.

OTHER THEATRE INCLUDES: Harper Regan, The Hothouse, Pillars of the Community (National); Testing the Echo, King of Hearts (Out of Joint); Love and Money, Senora Carrar's Rifles (Young Vic); Much Ado About Nothing (redesign, RSC/Novello); A Few Good Men (Haymarket); Dr Faustus (Chichester Festival Theatre); The Magic Carpet (Lyric Hammersmith); Port, As You Like It, Poor Superman, Martin Yesterday, Fast Food, Coyote Ugly (Royal Exchange, Manchester); Night of the Soul (RSC/Barbican); Under the Curse, Eyes of the Kappa (Gate); Crime & Punishment in Dalston (Arcola); Search & Destroy (New End); The Whore's Dream (RSC/Edinburgh).

Ian is Head of Sound at the Royal Court.

KATE GILLESPIE (Fate)

THEATRE INCLUDES: Hairspray (Shaftesbury Theatre); Tender Dearly (West Yorkshire Playhouse); The Legend of the Lion King (Disneyland, Paris); Aladdin (Old Vic); Hair (Gate, Notting Hill); Nos Vie en Rose (Edinburgh Festival Fringe/ Birmingham Hippodrome); South Pacific (Grange Park Opera).

TELEVISION INCLUDES: Emmerdale.

KEVIN HARVEY (Rey-Rey)

THEATRE INCLUDES: Tartuffe (Rose/Liverpool Everyman); Stags & Hens (Royal Court Liverpool); Clockwork (National); Dr Faustus (Bristol Old Vic); Speaking Like Magpies, Sejanus: His Fall, Believe What You Will, Thomas Moore (RSC); Macbeth (Out Of Joint); The Key Game (Talawa); Souls (LTC); Raggamuffin (Ukarts).

TELEVISION INCLUDES: Spooks: Code 9, Adam & Shelley Show, Ruby in the Smoke, Holby City, Merseybeat, Everybody Loves Sunshine, The Lenny Henry Show, Hearts & Minds, Dancin' Thru the Dark, Sweet Soul Harmonies, The Golden Collar.

FILM INCLUDES: A Boy Called Dad, Salvage, Till Death.

RADIO INCLUDES: Cavalry, Brief Lives, Fused Ricebowl, The Book of Love, The Morning After, Why Don't You Stop Talking?.

NATALIE IBU (Assistant Director)

AS ASSISTANT DIRECTOR FOR THE ROYAL COURT: The Girlfriend Experience.

AS DIRECTOR, THEATRE INCLUDES: The Red Shoes Re-heeled (Royal Lyceum Youth Theatre, Edinburgh); We Were . . . Re-imagining the Mother (G12, Glasgow); We Were... In Development (Citizens, Glasgow); We Were . . . in a Cafe (Gramofon, Glasgow); Say What… (Arches Scratch, Glasgow); I Know All the Secrets in My World . . . (Contact, Manchester); Women's Voices (NewWriting NewWorlds, Glasgow); Hang Up, Lesson Learned (Citizens' Young Co., Glasgow); Blooded (Fresh Perspectives, Mansfield); Road (De Montfort University, Leicester).

AS ASSISTANT DIRECTOR, THEATRE INCLUDES: Zameen (Kali Theatre, London); Fugee (Royal Lyceum Youth Theatre, Edinburgh); Peter Pan, Desire Under the Elms (Citizens', Glasgow); The Shadow of a Pie (Lung Ha's Theatre Co., Edinburgh); The Ghost Downstairs, The Butterfly Lion (New Perspectives Theatre Co., East Midlands).

Natalie is Trainee Director at the Royal Court, supported by ITV under the ITV Theatre Director Scheme.

ALEX LANIPEKUN (Eric)

THEATRE INCLUDES: Bugsy Malone (NYMT); Eyes Catch Fire (Finborough).

TELEVISION INCLUDES: Spooks (Regular), Talk To The Hand.

FILM INCLUDES: Crocodile, The Fourth Angel, Apples & Oranges.

RADIO INCLUDES: Kim's Game, The Rocking Horse, Nature Calls, The Devil Was Here Yesterday, Dr Zhivago, Fortunes of War, Charles Paris, The Picture Man, Tomorrow Today, Donation, The Doppler Effect.

AWARDS INLCUDE: Carlton Hobbs Award 2007.

LEON LOPEZ (Deity)

THEATRE INCLUDES: Piaf (Donmar); Rent (Duke of York's); Chitty Chitty Bang Bang (UK Tour); Strictly Motown, Drums of Anfield (Neptune); In My Country Devils Are White (Liverpool Arts Centre); Macbeth (Liverpool Everyman).

TELEVISION INCLUDES: Hollyoaks in the City, The Bill, Court Room, Holby City, Merseybeat, Brookside.

MANWE (Choreographer)

AS CHOREOGRAPHER: Debelah Morgan (US Tour); Chris Maorsoul (US Tour); Deep Soul Poets (US Tour), Lady GaGa (US Tour & Just Dance Video); Danity Kane (US Tour); Jojo (US Tour); Emily King (US Tour); Amerie (US Tour/I Thing Music Video), Damita Jo (Janet Jackson).

AS DANCER: Savage Jazz Company, Berkeley City Ballet, Lose My Breath (Destiny's Child Music Video), Fashion Rocks (Black Eyed Peas), Michael Jackson 30th Anniversary Special, Brit Awards 2004 (Gwen Stefani, Missy Elliott, Alicia Keys) Amerie 2003 US Tour, 2003 MTV Music Awards (Beyonce).

HOLLY QUIN-ANKRAH (Fay)

TELEVISION INCLUDES: Massive, Shameless, Rock Rivals, Grange Hill.

DANNY SAPANI (Lucian)

FOR THE ROYAL COURT: Neverland.

OTHER THEATRE INCLUDES: Radio Golf (Tricycle); Big White Fog (Almeida); The Overwhelming, Antony and Cleopatra, The Machine Wreckers, Richard II, His Dark Materials (National); Macbeth (Arcola & International Tour); To the Green Fields and Beyond (Donmar); Julius Caesar (Globe); The Silver Lake (Wilton's Music Hall); Measure for Measure (Nottingham Playhouse); Julius Caesar (Royal Exchange); Measure for Measure (Cheek by Jowel Tour); The Lion (Talawa); Love at a Loss (Wild Iris); The Beggar's New Clothes (Cockpit); The Honest Whore (Boulevard Theatre).

TELEVISION INCLUDES: Place of Execution, The Bill, Holby Blue, Blue Murder, Little Britain, Holby City, Serious and Organised, In Deep, Ultimate Force, Fish, Trial & Retribution, Shakespeare Shorts, Casualty, Richard II, Stick With Me Kid, Between The Lines, B & B Henry.

FILM INCLUDES: The Oxford Murders, Song for a Raggy Boy, Anansi, Timecode II, Going Down the Road.

ALEX SILVERMAN (Musical Director)

THEATRE SCORES INCLUDE: Cloudcuckooland (UK Tour); Romeo & Juliet, Much Ado About Nothing (Globe); Othello (Salisbury Playhouse); Richard III (Southwark); The Sweet Science of Bruising (National Studio); Crunch (West End); Pete & Dud: Come Again (UK Tour).

AS MUSICAL DIRECTOR/CHORUS MASTER: Eurobeat (West End/UK Tour); Certified Male (Assembly); Bridgetower (City of London Festival); At the Drop of a Hippopotamus (Pleasance/UK Tour); David Benson's Christmas Party (Bloomsbury Theatre/UK Tour); Dick Whittington (Newbury Corn Exchange); Swallow Song (Oxford Playhouse); Hamlet! The Musical (Far Eastern Tour).

OTHER MUSIC WORK INCLUDES: Alex has written music for BBC Radio, Channel 4 and Artsworld TV, and worked with a broad range of artists and ensembles, including the English Touring Opera and the band Hot Chip.

CRAIG STEIN (Venus)

THEATRE INCLUDES: Rent (Duke Of York's); Wicked (Apollo-Original London Cast); Oliver (Palladium); Carousel (National).

TELEVISION INCLUDES: Holby City, Down To Earth, Casualty, Eastenders.

FILM INCLUDES: The Prodigals.

NATHAN STEWART-JARRETT (Wilson / Nina)

THEATRE INCLUDES: The History Boys (National Tour/Wyndham's); Big White Fog, A Chain Play (Almeida); The Little Foxes (Perth Rep); Sweet Bird of Youth (Dundee Rep), Brixton Stories (Lyric Hammersmith).

TELEVISION INCLUDES: Apples & Oranges, Casualty.

ULTZ (Designer)

FOR THE ROYAL COURT: The Good Family, The Khomenko Family Chronicles, The Winterling, Stoning Mary, A Girl in a Car with a Man, Fresh Kills, The Weather, Bear Hug, Bone, Fallout, The Night Heron, Fireface, Lift Off, Mojo (& Steppenwolf, Chicago).

RECENT DESIGNS INCLUDE: The Harder They Come (Theatre Royal Stratford East/Barbican/Playhouse Theatre); The Ramayana (National); Hobson's Choice, A Respectable Wedding (Young Vic); The Gods are Not to Blame, The Estate (Tiata Fahodzi); The Bitter Tears of Petra Von Kant (ENO & Theater Basel), Cavalleria Rusticana, I Pagliacci (ENO); Macbeth (Glyndebourne).

AS DIRECTOR & DESIGNER: Summer Holiday (Blackpool Opera House/ Hammersmith Apollo/ UK tour/ South African tour); Jesus Christ Superstar (Aarhus/Copenhagen); Don Giovanni, Cosi fan tutte (in Japanese for Tokyo Globe); A Midsummer Night's Dream (National Arts Centre, Ottawa); The Blacks (co-directed, Market Theatre, Johannesburg/ Stadsteater, Stockholm); The Screens (California); The Maids, Deathwatch (co-directed RSC); Perikles (Stadsteater, Stockholm); Snowbull (Hampstead); The Blacks Remixed (co-directed with DJ Excalibah), The Public, The Taming of the Shrew, Pericles, Baiju Bawra, Da Boyz, Pied Piper – A Hip Hop Dance Revolution (all as Associate Artist at Theatre Royal Stratford East).

AWARDS INCLUDE: 2007 Olivier Award for Outstanding Achievement in an Affiliate Theatre for Pied Piper.

JESSIKA WILLIAMS (Faith)

THEATRE INCLUDES: The Bacchae (National Theatre of Scotland); The Last Days of Judas Iscariot (Almeida); Such Is Nature (Cat In A Cup); Beowulf (Arches); Thérèse Raquin (Citizens, Glasgow).

TELEVISION INCLUDES: Dr Who, Taggart.

FILM INCLUDES: The Descent II, Immeasurable Joy, Contorted Hazel.

CHAHINE YAVROYAN (Lighting)

FOR THE ROYAL COURT: Relocated, The Wonderful World of Dissocia (National Theatre of Scotland tour), The Lying Kind, Almost Nothing, At the Table, Iron (& Traverse), Bazaar, Another Wasted Year.

OTHER THEATRE INCLUDES: Three Sisters (Manchester Royal Exchange); Dallas Sweetman (Paines Plough at Canterbury Cathedral), Fall, Damascus (Traverse), God in Ruins (RSC/Soho), Il Tempo Del Postino (Manchester International Festival), How to Live (Barbican), Realism (Edinburgh International Festival), Mahabharata (Sadlers' Wells).

DANCE INCLUDES: Jasmin Vardimon Dance, Bock & Vincenzi, Frauke Requardt, Colin Poole, CanDoCo, Ricochet.

MUSIC WORK INCLUDES: Plague Songs (Barbican Hall), Dalston Songs (Linbury Studio), Death of Klinghoffer (Edinburgh International Festival), Jocelyn Pook Ensemble.

SITE SPECIFIC WORK INCLUDES: Enchanted Parks (Newcastle), Dreams of a Winter Night (Belsay Hall), Deep End (Marshall St. Baths), Ghost Sonata (Sefton Park, Palmhouse)

THE ENGLISH STAGE COMPANY AT THE ROYAL COURT

'For me the theatre is really a religion or way of life. You must decide what you feel the world is about and what you want to say about it, so that everything in the theatre you work in is saying the same thing ... A theatre must have a recognisable attitude. It will have one, whether you like it or not.'

George Devine, first artistic director of the English Stage Company: notes for an unwritten book.

photo: Stephen Cummiskey

As Britain's leading national company dedicated to new work, the Royal Court Theatre produces new plays of the highest quality, working with writers from all backgrounds, and addressing the problems and possibilities of our time.

"The Royal Court has been at the centre of British cultural life for the past 50 years, an engine room for new writing and constantly transforming the theatrical culture" Stephen Daldry

Since its foundation in 1956, the Royal Court has presented premieres by almost every leading contemporary British playwright, from John Osborne's *Look Back in Anger* to Caryl Churchill's *A Number* and Tom Stoppard's *Rock 'n' Roll*. Just some of the other writers to have chosen the Royal Court to premiere their work include Edward Albee, John Arden, Richard Bean, Samuel Beckett, Edward Bond, Jez Butterworth, Martin Crimp, Ariel Dorfman, Christopher Hampton, David Hare, Eugène Ionesco, Ann Jellicoe, Terry Johnson, Sarah Kane, David Mamet, Martin McDonagh, Conor McPherson, Joe Penhall, Mark Ravenhill, Simon Stephens, Wole Soyinka, Polly Stenham, David Storey, debbie tucker green, Arnold Wesker and Roy Williams.

"It is risky to miss a production there" Financial Times

In addition to its full-scale productions, the Royal Court also facilitates international work at a grass roots level, developing exchanges which bring young writers to Britain and sending British writers, actors and directors to work with artists around the world. The Royal Court Young Writers' Programme also works to develop new voices with their bi-annual Festival and year-round development work for writers under the age of 26.

"Yes, the Royal Court is on a roll. Yes, Dominic Cooke has just the genius and kick that this venue needs... It's fist-bitingly exciting." Independent

PROGRAMME SUPPORTERS

The Royal Court (English Stage Company Ltd) receives its principal funding from Arts Council England, London. It is also supported financially by a wide range of private companies, charitable and public bodies, and earns the remainder of its income from the box office and its own trading activities.

The Genesis Foundation supports the Royal Court's work with International Playwrights.

The Jerwood Charity supports new plays by new playwrights through the Jerwood New Playwrights series.

The Artistic Director's Chair is supported by a lead grant from The Peter Jay Sharp Foundation, contributing to the activities of the Artistic Director's office. Over the past ten years the BBC has supported the Gerald Chapman Fund for directors.

**ROYAL COURT
DEVELOPMENT
ADVOCATES**
John Ayton
Anthony Burton
Sindy Caplan (Vice Chair)
Cas Donald
Allie Esiri
Celeste Fenichel
Stephen Marquardt
Emma Marsh
Mark Robinson
William Russell (Chair)

PUBLIC FUNDING
Arts Council England, London
British Council
London Challenge

CHARITABLE DONATIONS
American Friends of the Royal Court Theatre
Bulldog Prinsep Theatrical Fund
Gerald Chapman Fund
Columbia Foundation
The Sidney & Elizabeth Corob Charitable Trust
Cowley Charitable Trust
The Edmond de Rothschild Foundation*
The Dorset Foundation
The D'Oyly Carte Charitable Trust
E*TRADE Financial
Esmée Fairbairn Foundation
The Edwin Fox Foundation
Francis Finlay*
The Garfield Weston Foundation
Genesis Foundation
Haberdashers' Company
Jerwood Charitable Foundation
John Thaw Foundation
Kudos Film and Televisoin
Lloyds TSB Foundation for England and Wales
Dorothy Loudon Foundation*

Lynn Foundation
John Lyon's Charity
The Laura Pels Foundation*
The Martin Bowley Charitable Trust
Paul Hamlyn Foundation
The Peggy Ramsay Foundation
Quercus Charitable Trust
Jerome Robbins Foundation*
Rose Foundation
Royal College of Psychiatrists
The Royal Victoria Hall Foundation
The Peter Jay Sharp Foundation*
Sobell Foundation
Wates Foundation

SPONSORS
BBC
Dom Perignon
Links of London
Pemberton Greenish
Smythson of Bond Street

BUSINESS BENEFACTORS & MEMBERS
Grey London
Hugo Boss
Lazard
Merrill Lynch
Vanity Fair

INDIVIDUAL SUPPORTERS

ICE-BREAKERS
Act IV
Anonymous
Ossi and Paul Burger
Mrs Helena Butler
Cynthia Corbett
Shantelle David
Charlotte & Nick Fraser
Mark & Rebecca Goldbart
Linda Grosse
Mr & Mrs Tim Harvey-Samuel
David Lanch
Colette & Peter Levy

Watcyn Lewis
David Marks
Nicola McFarland
Janet & Michael Orr
Pauline Pinder
Mr & Mrs William Poeton
The Really Useful Group
Lois Sieff OBE
Gail Steele
Nick & Louise Steidl

GROUND-BREAKERS
Anonymous
Moira Andreae
Jane Attias*
Elizabeth & Adam Bandeen
Philip Blackwell
Mrs D H Brett
Sindy & Jonathan Caplan
Mr & Mrs Gavin Casey
Carole & Neville Conrad
Clyde Cooper
Andrew & Amanda Cryer
Robyn M Durie
Hugo Eddis
Mrs Margaret Exley CBE
Robert & Sarah Fairbairn
Celeste & Peter Fenichel
Andrew & Jane Fenwick
Ginny Finegold
Wendy Fisher
Hugh & Henri Fitzwilliam-Lay
Joachim Fleury
Lydia & Manfred Gorvy
Richard & Marcia Grand*
Nick & Catherine Hanbury-Williams
Sam & Caroline Haubold
Nicholas Josefowitz
David P Kaskel & Christopher A Teano
Peter & Maria Kellner*
Mrs Joan Kingsley & Mr Philip Kingsley
Mr & Mrs Pawel Kisielewski
Varian Ayers and Gary Knisely
Rosemary Leith
Kathryn Ludlow
Emma Marsh

Barbara Minto
Gavin & Ann Neath
Mark Robinson
Paul & Jill Ruddock
William & Hilary Russell
Jenny Sheridan
Anthony Simpson & Susan Boster
Brian D Smith
Carl & Martha Tack
Katherine & Michael Yates

BOUNDARY-BREAKERS
John and Annoushka Ayton
Katie Bradford
Tim Fosberry
Edna & Peter Goldstein
Reade and Elizabeth Griffith
Sue & Don Guiney
Rosanna Laurence
Jan and Michael Topham

MOVER-SHAKERS
Anonymous
Dianne & Michael Bienes*
Lois Cox
Cas & Philip Donald
John Garfield
Duncan Matthews QC

HISTORY-MAKERS
Jack & Linda Keenan*
Miles Morland
Ian & Carol Sellars

MAJOR DONORS
Daniel & Joanna Friel
Deborah & Stephen Marquardt
Lady Sainsbury of Turville
NoraLee & Jon Sedmak*

*Supporters of the American Friends of the Royal Court

FOR THE ROYAL COURT

Royal Court Theatre, Sloane Square, London SW1W 8AS
Tel: 020 7565 5050 Fax: 020 7565 5001
info@royalcourttheatre.com, www.royalcourttheatre.com

Artistic Director **Dominic Cooke**
Associate Directors **Ramin Gray***, **Sacha Wares**⁺
Associate Director (Maternity Cover) **Jeremy Herrin**
Artistic Associate **Emily McLaughlin**
Associate Producer **Diane Borger**
Diversity Associate **Ola Animashawun***
Education Associate **Lynne Gagliano***
Trainee Director (ITV Scheme) **Natalie Ibu**‡
Personal Assistant to the Artistic Director **Victoria Reilly**

Literary Manager **Ruth Little**
Literary Associate **Terry Johnson***
Senior Reader **Nicola Wass****
Pearson Playwright **Daniel Jackson**†
Literary Assistant **Marcelo Dos Santos**

Associate Director International **Elyse Dodgson**
International Administrator **Chris James**
International Assistant **William Drew**

YWP Manager **Nina Lyndon**
Writers' Tutor **Leo Butler**
YWP Support Worker **Clare McQuillan***

Casting Director **Amy Ball**
Casting Assistant **Lotte Hines**

Head of Production **Paul Handley**
JTU Production Manager **Sue Bird**
JTU Production Manager (Maternity Cover) **Tariq Rifaat**
Production Assistant **Sarah Davies**
Head of Lighting **Matt Drury**
Lighting Deputy **Nicki Brown**
Lighting Assistants **Stephen Andrews, Katie Pitt**
Head of Stage **Steven Stickler**
Stage Deputy **Duncan Russell**
Stage Chargehand **Lee Crimmen**
Chargehand Carpenter **Richard Martin**
Head of Sound **Ian Dickinson**
Sound Deputy **David McSeveney**
Head of Costume **Iona Kenrick**
Costume Deputy **Jackie Orton**
Wardrobe Assistant **Pam Anson**
Sound Operator **Alex Caplan**

ENGLISH STAGE COMPANY

President
Sir John Mortimer CBE QC

Vice President
Dame Joan Plowright CBE

Honorary Council
Sir Richard Eyre CBE
Alan Grieve CBE
Martin Paisner CBE

Executive Director **Kate Horton**
Head of Finance and Administration **Helen Perryer**
Planning Administrator **Davina Shah**
Senior Finance and Administration Officer **Martin Wheeler**
Finance Officer **Rachel Harrison***
Finance and Administration Assistant **Tessa Rivers**
Interim Personal Assistant to the Executive Director
Frances Marden

Head of Communications **Kym Bartlett**
Marketing Manager **Becky Wootton**
Press Officer **Stephen Pidcock**
Audience Development Officer **Gemma Frayne**
Audience Development Assistant **Ruth Hawkins**
Sales Manager **Kevin West**
Deputy Sales Manager **Daniel Alicandro**
Box Office Sales Assistants **Ed Fortes, Shane Hough,
Ciara O'Toole**

Head of Development **Jenny Mercer**
Development Manager **Hannah Clifford**
Development Officer **Lucy James**
Development Assistant **Penny Saward**

Theatre Manager **Bobbie Stokes**
Front of House Manager **Claire Simpson**
Deputy Theatre Manager **Daniel O'Neill**
Duty Manager **Stuart Grey***
Café Bar Managers **Paul Carstairs, Katy Mudge**
Head Chef **Stuart Jenkyn**
Bookshop Manager **Simon David**
Assistant Bookshop Manager **Edin Suljic***
Bookshop Assistant **Emily Lucienne**
Building Maintenance Administrator **Jon Hunter**
Stage Door/Reception **Simon David***, **Paul Lovegrove,
Tyrone Lucas**

Thanks to all of our box office assistants, ushers and bar staff.
+ Sacha Wares' post is supported by the BBC through the Gerald Chapman Fund.
** The post of Senior Reader is supported by NoraLee and Jon Sedmak through the American Friends of the Royal Court Theatre.
‡ The post of Trainee Director is supported by ITV under the ITV Theatre Director Scheme.
† This theatre has the support of the Pearson Playwrights' scheme, sponsored by the Peggy Ramsay Foundation.
* Part-time.

Council
Chairman **Anthony Burton**
Vice Chairman **Graham Devlin**

Members
Jennette Arnold
Judy Daish
Sir David Green KCMG
Joyce Hytner OBE
Stephen Jeffreys
Phyllida Lloyd
James Midgley
Sophie Okonedo
Alan Rickman
Anita Scott
Katharine Viner
Stewart Wood

Tarell Alvin McCraney
Wig Out!

faber and faber

First published in 2008
by Faber and Faber Limited
74-77 Great Russell Street, London, WC1B 3DA

Typeset by Country Setting, Kingsdown, Kent CT14 8ES
Printed by CPI Group (UK) Ltd, Croydon, CR0 4YY

A CIP record for this book
is available from the British Library

ISBN 978-0-571-24592-5

FSC
www.fsc.org
MIX
Paper from
responsible sources
FSC® C013604

6 8 10 9 7

For

Donnie *aka* Kimberly Armani

and

Xavier

and

Derick

Wig Out! was made possible by generous support from The Yale School of Drama, Richard Nelson and Karen Hartman and the immense company of actors, directors, dramaturges and artistic staff at the Sundance Summer Theater Lab, 2007

Author's Note

I wrote *Wig Out!* firstly because the ballroom scene became a way for me to explore how all marginalised communities – in an effort to thwart modernity or the centre of societies – push out to the fringes and create hierarchies within themselves. And those structures become the way they judge, marginalise and elevate each other. They rework rules and create their own cosmology.

In other words, I was like: 'It is *fucking amazing* how people who are transgender gay and "other" find a way to make everything glamorous and powerful and magical and dangerous and costly for one night.' *Everything* is on the line at A DRAG BALL.

During the day, one might get stared at, called a name on a street corner or, worse, accosted by someone outside the circle, but for that night at the ball one could be literally the *queen of it all*. The next day, it's all back to being 'queer'. It was heavy and hard and beautiful and heroic.

This is a story about how drag houses can be like 'the home you never had or the home you never wanted'. It's the bonds of the house that make people family, but – just like family – they can be dysfunctional. More often than not, the people coming to join a drag house are already hurt and scared from their own homes, and they bring those wounds into their new family.

But it's also about love. And loving someone fully. No matter what they are or who they are. How do you love someone who feels like they are in the wrong body? How do you love someone who is fem but is supposed to be, in the eyes of the world, masculine? How do you love someone who doesn't love you back?

Specifically this is the House of Lights' story, although we watch it through the lens of Eric. They are the meetings of the two worlds for us: the world of the drag houses – which we are less familiar with – and the world of gay life to which pop culture is becoming quickly acclimatised.

But are they ready for queer life of colour?

A hero of mine once said that black men loving each other was a revolutionary act. Something about that still resounds in my mind and heart. So . . .

Come for the party, stay for the heartbreak.
Come for the ball, and be careful it doesn't drop on you.

Tarell Alvin McCraney

Characters

THE HOUSE OF DIABOLIQUE

Serena
a man in his late twenties, early thirties,
Mother of the House of Diabolique

Loki
a young white man in his late teens,
a part of the House of Diabolique

Eric
The Red, a handsome man of colour,
light in complexion, twenties

WIG OUT!

Notes

Stage directions in italics are to be played.

Other stage directions are to be spoken and played.

Italicised lines indicate songs.

Speech prefixes without following dialogue
are silent actions and hold a rhythm.

Act One

Faith (*over the loudspeaker*)
Welcome to the Royal Court production
Of *Wig Out!* Please feel
Free, now, to turn off all pagers, cellphones, watch alarms and
Anything that might disturb these children while
Performing. Trust me, If you knew how bad they would
Read you if one went off. And now for your listening pleasure . . . the Fates Three!

SCENE ONE

In darkness we hear the Fates before we
See them. They loud, girl! Loud! They sing
A train-like melody throughout the scene. They
should feel free to 'go head be grown with it'
When the spirit moves them. We hear
A train moving through a tunnel.

The Fates Three
Movin
Movin
Movin
Always
Movin
Gotta keep movin
Always movin
Movin
Movin
Gotta keep movin

Always movin
Movin
Movin
STOP!

Fay
Lights up on Wilson . . .

They stare at her . . .

I mean Miss Nina looking fierce and
Forward.

Fate
Bing-bong!

Faith
Doors closing!

The Fates Three (*singing train-like melody*)
Stop!

Fate
Enter Eric.

Fay
Oh yessir!

Faith
Make your mouth drop like –

All (*except Eric*)
What the fu—!

Fate
He sits across from Ms Nina.

The Fates Three
Huh.

Singing train-like melody.

Stop!

Fay
Errrrr!

Breaks squeal.

Fate (*to Fay*)
Ooh girl!

Fay
Sorry, Fate . . .

Fate
It's alright, Fay . . .

Faith
Attention passengers.
We are stopped waiting for signals ahead.
Signals to come and go.
The train will be moving again
Hopefully, shortly.

Nina (*to Eric*)
Hello.

Eric

Nina
Where you coming from?

Faith
The hum of the train.

Nina
Where you going?

Faith
The blink of the lights.

Nina
I could take you there . . . I could
Go with you.

Fay
Eric looks out the window.

Nina
You're beautiful . . .

Fate
Beautiful . . . so beautiful . . .

Nina
Hey . . .

Fay
Stays facing the window.

Faith
Nina drops the fem diva.

Fate
Giving you all butch . . .

Wilson
Faggots.

Eric
What!

Fay
Smiles.

Fate
Bing-bong.

Faith
Doors closing.

The Fates Three sing train-like melody low and under.

Nina
Sorry, all my sweet talk wasn't
Working.

Eric
You need to watch your mouth

Nina/Wilson
Rather watch yours. /
You like boys?

Eric
What?

Nina
Are you into men?

Eric
You just gone say that . . .
Ask me that out like that?

Nina
I don't like to beat around bush.

Eric
I bet.

Wilson
I could love you.

Eric
I don't think I'm your type.

Wilson/Nina
You are . . .
Red, lean a real boy.
Like Pinocchio
Tell a lie so I can watch it grow.

Eric (*laughing*)
I don't think so.

Wilson
Think again. I might be he/she you seek.

Eric
I'm into men, man.

Each 'take away' during the following, Wilson removes a piece of drag.

Fay
A take away.

Eric
Uh?

Fay
A take away.

Eric
Eh!

Wilson
Huh?

Eric
You're in public!

Wilson
Oh, you're not into PDA?

Fay
A take . . .

Eric (*loud*)
Look I'm into other *men*!

The Fates Three
STOP!

Fay
Blush!

Fate
Bing-bong!

Faith
Doors closing.

The Fates begin, yes, again, girl!

Wilson

You a bottom right?

Eric

Eh!

Wilson

A passive . . .

Eric

I think I have embarrassed myself –

Wilson

You like thick dick!

Eric

– enough for one day.

He stands to move.

Wilson

What, you gone get off the train . . .
Don't do that, it's still movin'!
I mean if you are going to commit suicide, guy,
Let me at least hold the door for you.

Eric smiles.

What happened? You just remember heaven, Angel?
Look at all those teeth. You putting a spell on me with
    that smile.
'Oh you hurtin' that!'

Eric

You're good.

Wilson

I can show you better.

The Fates sing faster, louder.

Eric
I'm Eric.

Wilson
Erin?

Eric
Eric!

Wilson
It's hard to hear you through the noise.
Come closer.

Eric
Eric! What's your name?

Wilson
When?

Eric
Quinn?

Wilson
Wilson!

Eric
That's your first name or your . . .

Wilson
Why?

Eric
I just . . .

Wilson
What!

Eric
I wanna know your . . .

Wilson (*loud*)
Huh?

The Fates Three
STOP!

Eric
I wanna know your name if we gone fuck!

The Fates Three
LIGHTS!

A PROCESSIONAL

Faith
Passengers please check your
Surrounding areas.

Fate
The carriage ride is now . . .

The Fates Three
Ovah!

Faith
We travel as quick as we can . . .

Fay
Under the rainbow . . .

Fate
CAREFUL!

Fay
It ain't safe.
It's giving realness!

Faith
The thump!

Fate
Thud.

Fay
Thunder!

Faith
Music of Houses.

Fay
Calling you to . . .

The Fates Three
'Walk for me
Walk for me
Walk, walk, walk, walk, walk for me . . .'

Here –

Fay
Lives only glamour –

Fate
The only life!

Fay *and* **Fate**
The *only*!

The Fates Three
Here.

Faith
Vogue is the official language.

Fate
Old way . . .

Fay
New way . . .

The Fates Three
Kick!

Faith
Stonewall has come crumbling down.

Fate
And Paris is still burning.

Faith
We shop Limelight, for mimosa.

Fay
The ride here goes up –

Fate *and* **Fay**
Up –

The Fates Three
Up!!

Faith
In this gossamer and laced reality
There is never a moment
To be without your face . . .
To not be together . . .

Fay
One false move –

Faith
And you'll get . . .

The Fates Three
Chopped!

Fate
Here.

Faith
Where one night can leave you legendary –

Fay
Or a subsidiary . . .

Fate *and* **Fay**
Here.

Faith

Where a daughter that once was a son . . .

Fay

Can find family.

Faith

So as delicately as we can bring you . . .

Fay

A story of a House . . .

Faith

That was never quite a home.

Fay

Enter –

The Fates Three

THE HOUSE OF LIGHT!

SCENE TWO

A burst of light flares upstage and near 'bout blinds
The kids in the audience. From that direction,
Thinking upstage or maybe through the aisle
Of the theatre, you feel it? Comes the entire
House of Light: I'm talking Lucian the Father,
Rey-Rey the mother, Deity the DJ, Venus
The face, Nina the first child, followed by the Fates Three.
They rest in what seems to be a parlour with Rey-Rey
Sitting still and centre painting a family portrait
Not dissimilar to the Corleone family only fierce
And fashion-savvy. The lights go to black, in this
Tableau. Deity and Nina exit. When lights come up Loki,
Wearing his gothic apparel with a clown-tear tattoo
On his face, stands centre. An overly-tanned Twink
Of a man with his hair spiked and bleached black,
He argues with Rey-Rey, Mother of the House of Light.

22

Rey-Rey
Honey, look . . .

Loki
No, bitch!

Rey-Rey
Did you just . . .

Faith
I think he did!

Rey-Rey
Did you say . . .

Fay
She *said*, girl.

Rey-Rey
Loki, I know you didn't march your murky self
Up in my house meeting . . . Help me somebody.

Fates
Un –

Rey-Rey
– announced.

Fates
Un –

Rey-Rey
– asked for.
And then got the nerve to call me . . .

Venus
Uh, uh.

Rey-Rey
Let a 'bitch' acquaint you to where you've
Come. This is the House of Light! The house you left,
    Loki.

I am the Mother of this House. When you drag your narrow
Up in here you make sure you show some respect.

Loki

I have a message . . .

Lucian

Who's the message from?

Loki

From Serena, Mother of Diabolique,
To the Mother of Light, but seeing
How this sometimey queen wanna clown . . .

Rey-Rey

Clown? With that face you talk about clown?

Venus

Mama . . .

Rey-Rey

Giving you the *only* happy meal.

Lucian

Rey-Rey!

Rey-Rey

Old Ronald McDonald looking mother . . .

Lucian

Talk to me. I'm the father, you talk to me, Loki.

Loki

I know you the father, Lucian, but you better
Check these punks. I just come with a message.

Venus

You ain't gone have too many mo' messages serving
Like that to Legendary.

Loki

I don't give a fuck if Rey-Rey is legendary or not,

Venus. I don't. That's why I left this tired
House. Messy queens trying to keep this
Old way running, uh, uh. I give much respect and
No shade, but I'll fuck a bitch up legendary or
Otherwise. Try me.

Lucian

Even me, Loki? You fuck me up too?

Faith

He bites his lips.

Lucian

What? *Preguntas para ti Papi*. You gone fuck me up?

Fay

He cocks his head . . .

The Fates Three

He . . .

Rey-Rey

You better come on quick with this message, child.

Loki

The house of Diabolique is hosting the Cinderella Ball.

Fay

Say what?

Fate

Say huh?

Rey-Rey

She thinks she slick.

Loki

Oh then you understand me well, ancient one.
You bitches almost ain't make it out alive from
That last ball. What was that Shirley Caesar
We were giving last ball, girl?

Fay

It was Cheryl Pepsi

Loki

Shirley Caeser, Cheryl Pepsii, Laverne and Shirley . . .
Same stomach flu.

Rey-Rey

You tell Serena, Mother of the House of
Diabolique, that we understand the terms of
A Cinderella soirée and we will be there ready
To walk and win all that is ours. I hope your
Mucked up melancholy face beams previews
Of our presence, 'cause, bitch, after we come through
Gone be some blind and dazzled punks left in
The wake. So says the Mother of the House of
Light. Now run tell that!

Loki

Huh. I guess you said that.

Fay

Exit Loki, Trickster of the House of Diabolique.

Fate

Rey-Rey stares.

Lucian

What?

Rey-Rey

You let him disrespect me.

Lucian

He had message . . .

Rey-Rey

In front of my own house.

Lucian

Rey-Rey . . .

Rey-Rey
No, Lucian, what's going on?

Lucian (*shrugs*)
A ball.

Rey-Rey
You all up on him . . .

Lucian
Perate' Mami. Remember I do what and who the fuck
I please.

Faith
Enter Deity.

Deity
What's going on?

Venus
A Cinderella extravaganza!

Deity
Oh word!

Venus
Ooh, not excited.

Deity
You know I loves a good . . .

Lucian
Oh yeah?

Deity
'Cept with this nigga.

Lucian
Where the fuck were you?
It was a house meeting, Pa. Something
More important than your house, Deity?
You brought Ms Nina with you?

Deity
Nah, I don't know where she is . . .

Lucian
You in my face talking respect, Rey-Rey, there
You go, right there.
You call a house meeting and all your kids
Ain't here.
Mira tu casa, Mami, mira tu casa.

Deity
Lucian, I . . .

Lucian
Eh! Get ready for the ball.

Faith
Exit Lucian.

Fate
Father of Light.

Venus
He pissed now.

Deity
What's new? Nigga stay on me.

Faith
And you know why.

Deity
Huh.

Venus
You never let him get a lick of that
Chocolatey chew.

Deity
Eh girl! (*Pissed.*)

Rey-Rey
Children.

Faith

A mother smiles.

Fate

Pulling it together.

Rey-Rey

We Cinderellas must ready for a ball.

Shift.

Fate

Meanwhile . . .

Fay

Back in Nina's lair . . .

SCENE THREE

Fay

New lust sits . . .

Fate

Panting.

Lights up. Eric and Wilson lying in bed –
Post-coital, girl!

Eric

Wow!
That was hot.

Wilson

Mmm.
Can you hold me some more, Angel?

Eric

My name is Eric.

Wilson

Angel, let me call you butt-love.

Eric

Love?

Wilson

Eric

You've got these eyes . . .

Wilson

You can look into 'em all day?

Eric

No, I wish like hell you'd quit staring at me . . .
Making me nervous.

Wilson

Oh.

Eric

Like you're gonna eat me.

Wilson

Already have. I want seconds.

Eric

I leave myself wide open.

Wilson

And oh so well . . .

Eric

Damn it!

Wilson

It's okay . . . it's okay. I'm quick.

Eric

I'm hungry.

Wilson

If you lay back I will feed you.

Eric

Nah, listen. I'm hungry. Sex makes me hungry.

Wilson
Funny, sex makes me horny.
Like it feeds the fire it once quelled
So that what it undid, it did.

Eric
Damn, you are quick.

Wilson
Gotta be.

Eric
Hey are you . . .
You half Rican or something?

Wilson
Huh. You wonder why I cum in Spanish?

Eric
It just reminded me of something.

Wilson
Something good, I hope.

Eric
Mas bueno.

Wilson (*in his ear*)
Muy bien.

Eric
Ah, *Tito Puente* to you too.

Wilson (*laughing*)
You didn't like that?

Eric
I would like a little food in my belly.

Wilson
Be back.

Shift.

Watch this: the Fates are spread out across
The stage –Faith, Fate and Fay. As they break
The name of the house in three a spot beams
Down on them one by one. The music from
A soundtrack blares. The Fates begin to lip-sync and
Dance to the song with an ease. You can't believe,
Child. Finally, on the last lyric, the Fates forget
Steps, stumble and we realise this is just rehearsal.

The Fates Three
> HOUSE   OF   LIGHT!

> *Venus interrupts.*

SCENE FOUR

Venus
> Wait! Wait, wait . . . Ladies, cunties, whatever
> You like to be called. I mean this has got
> To give 'Sheila E' *glamorous life*. It's got to
> Have that old school, that new school, that
> No school. Your life is the dance feel . . .

Faith
> Uh . . .

Fay
> Debbie Allen . . .

Fate
> I'm tired.

Faith
> Me too.

Fay
Which category is this again?

Venus
Um. Soundtrack with a twist.

Faith
What's the twist?

Venus
You're fish, honey, real women.
Listen here, don't question art!

Fate
Why are we rehearsing this hard?

Fay
Okay! Venus, I love you girl, but you starting
To push a bitch.

Faith
When is the ball anyway?

Fay
She mumbles.

Venus
Tonight.

Fate
When?

Venus
Tonight.

Fate
Lies!

Fay
Propaganda.

Faith
Bitch who throws a ball in one night?

Enter Deity.

Deity
You don't know the story of Cinderella?

Venus
No, but I am sure you will tell us.

Deity
You used to like my stories.

Venus
Uh huh, they always put me right to sleep.

Deity
You sure it was the stories?

Venus
You have one night only.

The Fates Three
One night only!

Deity
The rules are the same. Each house is allowed to walk
All the categories set up, to strut they shit: fashion icon,
European runway, realness, the grand prize, but here
    comes
The catch.

Venus
The stakes are higher –

Deity
All the drag houses invited but half of them won't show.

Fay
Why?

34

Deity
Can't get it together in time. So only the
Strongest most skilful and legendary of houses
Will be there. And they have got to pull it, to win it.

Fate
This is fucked up!

Deity
Wh–what? Oh, we can rep light yo.

Venus
Always the optimist.

Deity
With these chicks singing and my baby running face.

Venus
I done told you 'bout calling me out my name . . .

Deity
I can have you calling my name in no time.

Faith
Excuse me, young and the restless, but how do we come
Out from all this shade?

Venus
Chile, please, Diabolique is one of the oldest Houses
     on the
Scene.

Fate
And old trees . . .

Fay
Give much shade.

Venus
Legend gives it that only the House of Octavian, those
Pigpen queens, were known for calling out a Cinderella
     ball.

Deity
You sure it was Octavian?

Venus
Negro, I told you the story.
How you trying to come for me!

Deity
I'm sorry, damn.

Venus
As I said, Octavian
Would work tirelessly like the umpa lumpas for Wonka
Crafting every category to fit they lil nasty needs so
That in the end they were sure to win. Until this one
Time Rey-Rey came into the ball. This is when she
Was walking House of Jameson, and she walked
Fashion icon!

Faith
What?

Venus
Left the kids gagging!

Deity
Left bitches De Gaga.

Venus *and* **Deity**
Degas.

Venus
Beat Serena the then-Diva of Octavian. And ever since,
Serena has had it in for Rey-Rey.
So that's the low-down down on this wild party.
We got till the stroke of midnight to get to hoppin'.

Fay
Wash the dishes!

Fate

Do the moppin'!

Venus

After that last ball girl we gotta win this. 'Cause
Whoever wins this comes out on top.
Like how I like it.

Fay

Yes, gurl!

Deity

Here she go on that shit again.

Venus

But see, you can put that out your mind, lil Deity blue.
Who, where, what I'm on top of is no longer a concern
    to you.

Deity

I was just playin'.

C'mon, girl, talk to me.

Venus

Not until you can act your age or
At least you're penis size.

Fay

Enter Rey-Rey.

Rey-Rey

Til 'em God o'mighty gonna shut you down!
Y'all do know I was raised COGIC,
Don't make me shout all over God's heaven!
You three harmonise.

The Fates Three

Hm.

Rey-Rey

Venus, love, get Ms Nina on the main line.

Venus
Oh, what? A bitch giving Verizon?
(*To Deity.*) Move!

Venus moves Deity aside and leaves.

Fay
The exit of love.

Rey-Rey (*to the Fates*)
Are they still broke up?

The Fates Three
Uh-huh.

Rey-Rey (*to Deity*)
Look at 'em.
Deity, baby, I have this brew that's gonna
Be a bash for the ball. Can you help me mix
The music? Can't work the tables like you
Youngins. Just so confusing and such.

Deity
Yes, ma'am.

Fate
A frown . . .

Faith
Turned upside down.

Deity offers the Mother of Light his arm – and what an arm!

Rey-Rey
Ooh chile, I have always enjoyed my
Second amendment, yes. The right to
Bare arms. Honey!

Rey-Rey and Deity exit.

A DREAM

Faith

Eric the Red
In his first Dream of Drag.

Sweetie Eric lies sleeping in Nina's bed.
While a dangerous dance/song plays
In his head. As it does Lil Loki with the tricked out
Hair comes into the space hitting various vogue
Poses and freaking us the fuck out. Behind him
Entering in a kimono, geisha-like in
The face (baby's face is beat!) is Mama Evil
Herself, Serena. She lips a song and gives
You ancient drama.

Loki strips some of Serena's outfit. Now she's in a
more modern dress.

More stripping, now she's in a skirt, no top. Holding
her chest.

Loki strips her further. Serena's now in a black leather
jockstrap. Loki exits. Lucian enters masked but bare
chested and dances pro–vok–actively! With Serena.

Lights out on Lucian and Serena doing
Unmentionable things honey.
Lights come up on the Fates in the corner.

SCENE FIVE

Faith

Eric, the Red, breathing heavy, wakes from his dream.

The sound of a phone ringing. Eric,
Disoriented, answers Nina/Wilson's phone.

Eric

Hello?

Lights come up on Venus.

Venus

Ooh, hello! How you doin'?
Is Miss Nina there?

Eric

Who! Oh . . . um . . . wait.
Who's . . . May I . . .

Venus

Oh no, may *I* ask . . .

Eric

Wilson's in the other . . .

Venus

That's okay because I asked to speak
To NI-NA.

Wilson (*off*)

Did you get that?
Eric?

Eric

I . . .

Wilson (*off*)

Who is it?

Eric

It's . . . It's . . .

Enter Wilson.

Wilson

Boy, gimme this!

Nina answers the phone.

Nina

What's the tea?

Venus

Mommy dearest wants to know
Why you insist on using wire hangers!

Nina

Venus, facey dear, beautiful mirror of us all
Tell me tonight was not the night to rehearse
For a ball.

Venus

I cannot tell a lie, yo ass is on the line.

Nina

Is she being shady? What's good?

Venus

The Diabolique's pulled it, gurl! Messy bitches
Called out a Cinderella ball.

Nina

You see that's why I don't play with trash,
Honey! Just tacky, Cliff, tacky. How long till
Take off?

Venus

Bitch, it's already high noon! Come on, Claire!
    I will just tell Mama . . .
Tell her you must've have been tied up.

Miss Nina

In traffic?

Venus

That too . . .

Venus *and* **Nina**

GET IN!

Nina hangs up, notices Eric is pulling on his pants.

Nina (*to Eric*)
Where you going?

Eric

Nina
I see Miss Kat has returned to snatch your tongue.

Eric

Wilson
You shouldn't eat so much, pussy boy,
Somebody might mistake you
For straight . . .

Eric
Huh. You, funny . . . I . . .

Wilson
Gotta go.

Eric
I have . . .

Wilson
A lot of work to do?

Eric
Stop that.

Wilson
If I do we won't get to the part where you close the
door behind you.

Eric
So, what, you kickin' me out?

Wilson
I've seen angels return to Heaven before.

Eric
I just . . .

Wilson

You're not this type of gay . . .
You don't usually say things like tea and talk the drag
    slang.

Eric

This . . . I had fun . . . I . . .
Huh, I did. I really . . .
This just . . .

Wilson

It scares you . . . this little ride I am giving you.
This introduction to two souls in one.
I know. But why don't you hold on for a while.
See what happens.
Earth isn't always so bad, Angel. It was once Paradise.

Someone ate some bad fruit and there we were
Naked and . . . lonely.

Eric

Wilson

You lonely, Angel?

Eric

Ain't we all?

Wilson

Where were you going . . . this morning on the train?

Eric

Nowhere. Home.

Wilson

Where were you coming from?

Eric

A club. I was supposed to meet somebody.

Wilson

Here I am.

Eric

Wilson

I live in that smile.

Eric

Wilson

Food's about ready, stay, let me feed you,
Then come and go with me to my father's house.

Shift.

INTERLUDE

*Yes Gurl! Venus enters the light dancing a
Cute two-step. You know nothing too much
But showing you that he could get loose if he
Needed to. Huh! The fates come in like a cute
Old-school core of back-up singers.*

Venus

Mi Abeula was Celia Cruz!

Faith

That's not how it goes, Venus!

Fay

Tell it right . . .

Venus

Mi Abuela wore a wig. The fiercest wigs. Everyday:
a new wig!
Gurl, we would come down to the house on the
weekends . . .

Fate

AY!

44

Venus

And there Grandma was, done up in a Faye Dunaway
or a short Doris
Day. And when we came to the door she would be like:

Fate

Venus!

Venus

Yes! She named me.

Faith

Venus is a girl name!

Venus

My mama said. Grandma
Said with a shrug:

Fate

'Huh, Venus with a penis. He's too beautiful
To be anything else.'

Fay

She didn't say that.

Venus

Honey would I lie . . .
About this?

Fate

Venus with a penis! Come in here to Grandma.
Let me dance with you.

Venus

And honey, we would get down.
Yes, ma'am. Get out there and she would let me wear
her
Open-toed shoes. honey, we'd get jazzy, yes, c'mon
Grandma, yes Grandma!
My mother would always sit back and watch,
She couldn't dance.

45

My grandmother wore a wig like all the abuelas from
Cuba did. She dug my dark skin. She couldn't stand
  my black-ass
Daddy 'cause he walked out on us. But loved my black
  within.
'Grandma I want to be just like you when I grow up!'

One day dancing with Grandma my mother bumped
  into
Me and I fell. I fell down.

Music out.

Fay
  Ankle turned.

Fate
  Face contorted.

Venus
  My grandma turned she looked at me and said,

Fate
  'Venus, get up. Levantante, be be.'

Venus
  I just looked at my mother.

Faith
  Stay down . . .

Venus
  Her eyes said.
  Eventually I got up but when I did,
  My grandma had taken off her wig.

Deity in front what looks like
A system girl, you know what I'm
Talking about, one them small grey
Silvery music-making, mixing things.
Talk to Ms Sets for more detail. Uh humph.
N E way, Deity stands playing an old
School joint. He rocks a little to the beat.
He then presses a button or mixes
A mix. Deity starts lip-rapping,
Flexing and dancing to
The music until of course Lucian
Enters the room.

Lucian
> Ah shit, Papi. *Que vo la!*
> I like this Deity, this that new shit.

Deity cuts the music.

Lucian
> Don't stop for me, Papi. You having fun?

Deity
> I was just . . .

Lucian
> You gonna walk realness rapper tonight?

Deity
> Just working on something for Rey-Rey.

Lucian
> Nah, nah, Rey be on that old shit. Keep us talking
> 'bout
> Some house music. House music almost got us
> chopped last
> Ball.

How you young sexy motherfuckas say
'True story?'

Deity

Yeah.

Lucian

With you out there, Deity, we ain't got to worry about
That tonight . . .

Deity

You know I don't walk no categories.

Lucian

Come here, Deity. We, me and you, its hard to
Um, talk man to man. So many faggots around.
But since you got into this House I ain't had a
Chance to, you know, really talk to you, Mijo.
You think we could talk?

Deity

Sure, man, what's on your mind?

Lucian

Aw man, you the only person who ask me
That! That's a relief. Usually everybody
Running to me telling me what they want.
You the only one ask Daddy what he wants.

Deity

Lucian

You smell good, Mijo. Damn, you look good –
You been working out?

Deity

I need to go talk to Venus.

Lucian

Eh man, sorry to hear about you breaking up.

Deity

Yeah, well, it happens.

Lucian

Must be lonely.
It's lonely on top.

Deity

Man, why don't you just say what you
Gone say?

Lucian

I don't have to say shit, uh? You know
What's up, Deity.

Deity

Look, Lucian . . .

Lucian

Call me Papi.

Deity

I just . . . I'm just trying
To rep my house, you know? Think 'bout
If me and you got down, then what?
What's next, me and the Fates? Be like a
House full of people I used to fuck. Who
Wants that . . . What kinda house would
That be? You feel me . . . Papi?

Lucian

Huh. Deity you . . . You gotta smart mouth.
Should put it to better use, feel me? Tonight
We gone need to pull out all the stops. I'm talking
About every category.

Deity

I gotcha on the turntables.

Lucian

The fuck! You the one who mixed that House
Shit for Rey-Rey last time. Hell no. You gone have to get

Out there and show some of that new Deity.
You know? Leave the faggots screaming for
You. Hm. Body realness and the grand prize. If
That's too much I understand. You know . . .

Deity

Lucian
I'll make it easy, say, no, don't worry about reppin'
Light ever again. I don't want that . . . I
Mean I would miss you. But it's on you.
I, uh, support you whatever you decide.
That some father shit to say right? Huh.

Faith
Thunder!

Sound of thunder.

Lucian
Damn . . . sounds like rain.

Fate
Distant thunder!

More thunder.

Lucian
See you in a lil bit . . . Mijo?

Deity
Yeah.

Lucian
Muy bien, Papo. Muy bien.

The Fates Three
Thunder!

End of Act One.

Act Two

Lights come up on Rey-Rey, Mother of the House,
In an upper room.
She stands almost naked looking mannish,
Or boyish. No drag, no wig. A black scarf wrapped
Around her head. She stands as if looking at herself
In a mirror. She takes the black scarf off to reveal a
Fully shaved head. Rey-Rey takes a breath. She
Sits at a make-up table. She begins with concealer.

Rey-Rey
When I was younger the kid next door, Jay,
Was my best friend in the whole world. Let's
Just say, as we got older we had artistic
Differences. To say the fucking least. Jay
Had an older brother . . . Anthony. To this day
I have yet to meet a man more beautiful than
Anthony. They lived . . . Jay and Ant, with their
Grandma. Dear ole Grandmamma Alice. Grandma
Wore a wig. Sometimes when Anthony started feelin'
Full of himself, smelling himself as my mother would
Say, he would throw on old Grandmamma's wig and
Impersonate her . . . to her face. He would stand in
    her wig . . .
Arms folded across his too-developed-for-fifteen chest
He would stare up grinning to Granny Alice's ageing
    face . . .
And act like she or how he perceived her to be.
'Anthony, stop that!' she would say, whispering through
Shame-founded lips. 'Cut that out. You do that too
    well.'
It was true . . .

He did.
He looked so beautiful in his grandmother's wig.
Young boys in wigs can be so beautiful.
Old women in wigs save some dignity.
Old men in toupees are funny . . .
But an old drag . . . an old queen in a crown. Huh.
Well . . .
Will you all . . . Will you all excuse me?

Lights go out on Rey-Rey.

SCENE ONE

Eric
Why is this so good?

Wilson
Your tongue's tasting it.

Eric
C'mon what you put in it?

Wilson
Love, affection, a splash of hot and lusty . . .

Eric
You silly . . .

Wilson
It's just like Lowry's 'cept sweeter.

Eric
Be for real.

Wilson
That's my problem. Soul fo' real.

Eric
Who . . .

Wilson
You don't remember them?

Wilson *and* **Eric**
Heavy D and who!
Soul fa real!

Eric
Yo, that's a throwback!

Wilson
Have you ever lov'd someone so much you die?

Eric
Wow. You should stick to cooking.

Wilson
Boy, I can sing. That was me playing.

Eric
See, you can't be fo' real.

Wilson
Please, it's my middle name.

Eric
Pharell.

Wilson
Earnest, you *nerd*.

Eric
Wilson Earnest . . .

Wilson
Ugly, huh? What's yours?

Eric
David.

Wilson
David. I like Angel Eric.

Eric

What's in it?

Wilson

Lay back.

Eric

K.

Wilson

Tell me what you taste . . .

Eric

Sweet.

Wilson

Eric

Nina/Wilson

Brown sugar water, hot, dark, mixed with cinnamon.
Don't get up. What else?

Eric

Butter . . .

Nina

Light cream butter and egg mixed good and together,
Mixed so it's one thing, so that is all together. Can't
Separate.

Eric

Bread.

Nina

Bread, old bread almost stale,
Near 'bout to throw it away. Rough bread
But cut it up. Slice it and see the inside still
Right.

Eric

Then . . .

Nina

Dip in the dark so the sweet soak in, then eye
Lash like brush with the creamy on top. Hold
The pan and throw it on hot so you can sear it
Soft over a licking fire. Too long will burn the
Bread, too little will mess up the sweet.

Eric

What else?

Nina

Hm?

Eric

There, there is something else . . . I can . . . I can taste it.

Nina

Aqua de Azucar from Puerto Rico.

Eric

Rum /

Nina

Hmm huh. Rum.
Is it . . . is it really good?

Eric

Yeah, it is. *Muy bien.*

SCENE TWO

Deity

And this cocksucker!
What was he threatening me?

Venus

Calm down . . .

Deity

I mean, it's just a drag house!

Venus
    To you . . .

Deity
    It don't put no food on my plate.

Venus
    I know.

Deity
    I almost went tick, tick boom on that kat!

Venus
    Deity . . .

Deity
    Don't call me that shit!

Venus
    That's your name.

Deity
    You know my name. Call me my name,
    Baby. I miss my name in your mouth.

Venus
    I'm not doing this with you today!

Deity
    What?

Venus
    We have a ball to get ready for . . . All
    He asked you to do was to walk a category.

Deity
    I don't wanna walk.

Venus
    OK, look, I need you to walk. We need
    To get in every category and pull a stunt
    And show, a shock and awe, even with your

Silly self we can do that. I'm gonna throw
Up in my mouth a little bit for saying this, but
Please?

Deity (*smiles*)
Huh.

Venus
What?

Deity
Don't you . . . Don't you miss this?
Me cutting up about something
And you calming me down? Us?

Venus
No.

Deity
I miss you.

Venus
Of course you do.
You're normal.

Deity
And you miss me too.

Venus
. . . So what.

Deity
Baby . . .

Venus
'Ve-nus.' 'Bitch.' 'You' . . . but not 'baby'.

Deity
Let's get back together.

Venus
You signing contracts and not reading
The fine print.

Deity

Long as you co-sign. I'm good.
Let's redo us.

Venus

You gonna let me do you?

Deity

Seems like everybody on my ass today.

Venus

Oh! So I'm like Lucian now?

Deity

No, but I'm saying we have fun without,
That right?

Venus

It's not all about fun. I told you when
We got together, Adrian, I said, I am not
Anybody's bottom girl. You get yours,
I get mine.

Deity

Eh, I take care of you.

Venus

Let me take care of you.

Deity

You do. Without . . .

Venus

I wanna fuck you, Adrian.
Not every day Not all day. Not today.
But if we gonna
Be . . . us, then that's a part of it. And if
You can't handle that . . . then . . .

Deity

I . . .

Venus

Adrian, no . . .

Deity

Love you.

Venus

I know you think you do.

Deity reaches out to Venus. She doesn't move.
He takes her hand. They walk off.

SCENE THREE

Wilson stands pulling on nylons
Over his underwear. Eric lays back.

Eric

So it's like a gang?

Wilson

No, Maria, this ain't *West Side Story.*

Eric

I'm trying to understand.

Wilson pulls on tight, obviously girl's jeans . . .

Wilson

What's to understand? You know
How families work or don't work. Ain't no
Book to explain it. There's a mother and
A father and the kids. And sometimes they
Get along and sometimes they don't.

Eric

But my mother and father ain't never make
Me dress up like a girl.

Wilson

Yeah, they made you dress up like a boy.

59

He synchs up a body suit.

They don't make me do anything. I came to
The house like this.

Eric
And they were like, 'cool'?

Wilson
They were like, 'Yes bitch! Fierce!'

The father named me.

Eric
What?

Wilson
He gave me a name.

Eric
Nina.

Wilson
Yeah . . .

Eric
Huh.

Wilson
What's wrong?

Eric
Maybe I shouldn't go with you.

Wilson
You scared to walk outside with me like this?

Eric
I'm just not used to it yet.

Wilson
Yet?

Eric

Wilson

I didn't know black boys could blush.
You like me.

Eric

No, I don't.

Wilson

Yes, you do.

Wilson pulls out a wig . . .

Eric

No, I don't.

Wilson

It wigs you out.

Eric

So in this ball do you get judged?

Wilson

Yup.

Eric

On what?

Wilson

How real you look or on how not real you look
Or on how classy or ghetto, I mean it depends
On the category.

Eric

What you get if they like you?

Wilson

Tens. Tens across the board.

Eric

And then you win the category?

Wilson
Mostly you get to say you won.

Eric
And if you don't win?

Wilson
You get chopped.

Eric
Like cut?

Wilson
Just as bad.

Eric
Damn, y'all are vicious.

Wilson
You don't know the half.

Eric
What do you walk?

Wilson
Huh. I guess not realness.

Eric
I mean no disrespect.

Wilson
I mostly perform. I impersonate.

Eric
You ever get chopped?

Wilson
I have been.

Eric
Were you upset?

Wilson
Yeah.

Eric

You cry?

Wilson

You wanna see me cry?

Eric

No.

Wilson

That's good.

Eric

What you doin?

Wilson puts the wig into a book bag.
He takes out a huge hood and
Some Timberland boots. He puts them on.

Wilson

You comfortable with me like this?

Eric

I can . . . I can handle that.

Wilson

Good. Here, carry this bag for me.

Eric

Alright.

Wilson

Just know when we get to the house I can't
Walk in like this.

Eric

Alright.

Wilson

You say alright now. Don't be getting all
Funny an' shit, acting brand new when I
Throw that wig on.

Faith
*Lights on the Fates Three standing topless facing
    downstage.
Holding their breasts. They sing until . . .*

SCENE FOUR

Fay
I don't know, girl.

Fate
Me neither.

Faith
The shit is a dilemma.

Fate
I mean, can't we just do it with
Clothes?

Faith
We could.

Fay
But would we win?

Fate
Okay, according to Lucian, no.

Faith
Chile, according to the truth, we wouldn't.

Fate
What is with the queers going gaga over
Girls gratis!

Faith
One of God's laws.

Fay
Titties fascinate everybody.

Faith (*to us*)
    You know how hard it is to be a girl –

The Fates Three
    A *real* girl!

Fay
    And win walks at the ball.

Faith
    It's like they got instant haterade for you.

Fay
    Yes ma'am. Just add queens and serve.

Fate
    We have this part . . .

Fay
    This piece . . .

Faith
    For the ball.

Faith
    Lucian wants us
    To drop our arms and show the world.

Fay
    So shady.

Fate
    But the kids will go up!

Fay
    I can just see them punks pounding the floor
    When I drop my arms and give them Fay D'jore.

The Fates Three
    Huh!

Rey-Rey (*off*)
    Don't walk away from me, Lucian Light.
    What the fuck did you say?

Lucian (*off*)
You heard what the fuck I said.

SCENE FIVE

The Fates Three
Rey-Rey and Lucian –

Fate
Coming down the stairs.

Faith
Screaming.

Rey-Rey
You trying to tell me? You trying
To say . . .

Lucian
I ain't trying to say
Nothing. I am telling you
Won't walk it not this night, no more
Nights. None.

Rey-Rey
And I am telling you!

Fay
And I am telling you!

Faith
Sang Effie.

Enter Deity and Venus.

Venus
What's going on now?

Faith
He moves to leave.

66

Rey-Rey

Hold the fuck on!

Fay

He grabs her wrist . . .

Fate

He presses her close . . .

The Fates Three

He . . .

Rey-Rey holds out her free hand, stopping Deity.

Rey-Rey

When this house was early light, low light,
I came in here and worked this bitch, you hear
Me. When it was not a time or place of glamour
In the scene I put the couture back in the bash.
That was my ass walking down with the true strut
Of fashion icon. I brought win after win and the name
Legendary to a house with little to know light until
There was Rey, there was no way, so even though I
May not have the glow of youth, motherfucker,
I got the glam of age. I know what it's like to try
To hold up fabulousness while everyone withers
And dies around you. I walked amongst the legends
Who didn't make it through. I lost most of my house to
An Aids war that the kids didn't know how to survive.

Faith

He rests.

Fay

Lets her go.

Rey-Rey

So even when HI-V came through here, laying waste
To my sisters, I survived, bitch. On that principle
Alone, out of respect for those who come before you,
Let me walk that walk, Lucian.

Lucian
Rey-Rey. *Lo siento*, Mommy. For your loss.
What you want me to do 'bout that? Listen to
Me thank you for bringing light legendary, uh.
But if you want to stay a legend you won't walk
This ball. I won't let you. Let it go.

Rey-Rey
If I lose, I step down.

Venus
What?

Faith
Rey-Rey girl!

Rey-Rey
If I lose . . .

Fay
Wait . . .

Fate
Stop.

Rey-Rey
If I get chopped in one category . . .

The Fates Three *and* **Venus**
Rey!

Rey-Rey
I will step down as acting Mother of the House of Light.

Fay
He cocks his head . . .

Fate
He steps back . . .

The Fates Three
He.

Rey-Rey

Lucian . . .

Lucian

I hear you, Mama. It's generous of you.

Rey-Rey

Well, you been wanting that for a lil while
Now, right? Someone younger, stronger, on
Your right come ball night reppin light.

Lucian

Okay, you walk fashionista tonight.
And if you lose . . .

Rey-Rey

I ain't giving up my house without a fight.

Lucian

But you heard me, though. *Si, Mami
De la Luz*? You hear me.

Lucian exits.

Rey-Rey

I hear you, love.
I hear you.

*Rey-Rey stands trying to hold
Strong, but when you realise love don't live
Here any more, there's little strength to stand
On and she crumbles a little and cries. Venus
And the Fates Three forgetting their modesty fall
Forward to hold their mother up but Rey-Rey shrugs off
Their help. She leads them out as they hum.
Deity is left alone on stage. The sound of rain.*

Deity
> My grandmother wore a wig. She died before I ever met
> Her. But my grandaddy, Pere, always kept her wig up
> On a Styrofoam holder next to his bed. Sometimes when
> I would sleep over my grandaddy's house
> I would hear him praying, talking to God, and then he
>> would
> In the smallest voice,
> That I could barely hear, I heard 'em say, 'I miss you
>> Mary, every day.
> I miss you and I love you.'
>
> My grandmother wore a wig. It sat in my grandfather's
>> room. We
> Would sit staring at it sometimes and he would tell me
> To treat women with respect, open
> Doors for them and say sweet things. 'When they gone,'
>> he say,
> You miss 'em, especially in the night, but even when
>> it's bright
> You miss them all day long.'
>
> A lotta women tried to marry my grandaddy. My daddy
> Even asked him if he wanted to start datin' again.
>> 'What for?'
> He say, 'I already got somebody who stands by me.
> I don't need nobody but who I gots with me.'
>
> *We see Wilson and Eric running in from the rain.*

Wilson
Go, go, go . . .

Eric
It just came out of nowhere.

Wilson
I know. I was sure those dark black
Clouds meant a dry night.

Eric
You wet.

Wilson
Yeah . . . you too.

Eric
Yeah.

Wilson
Huh.

Eric
We wet.

Wilson
Is . . . is my liner running?

Eric
You're wearing liner?

Wilson
Boy, I can't walk out the house without
Liner.

Eric
You sure you need it? What you hiding?

Wilson/Nina
Hiding? Its just there to / enhance the
Good and . . .

Eric
'Enhance the good.'

Wilson
Shut up. And conceal the bad.

Eric
Let me see?

He leans in close.

Wilson
Right here.

Eric
Right here?

He touches his face.

Wilson
Yeah.

Eric
Oh here.

Wilson (*laughing*)
Yes, boy.

Eric
And you put it on like
This . . .

He runs his finger . . .

Wilson
Yes.

Eric
Easy.

Wilson
Breezy . . .

Eric
Beautiful . . .

Venus (*off*)
Coloured girl!

SCENE SEVEN

Venus
Well, look what the tide dragged in.
And looking like a pirate of the Carib.
Bitch, you are good and late!

I assume this your tied-up.

Eric
I'm Eric.

Venus
I bet you are.

Eric
You must be Venus.

Venus
You recognise the voice?

Eric
And the attitude.

Venus
Ooh yes, ma'am, ain't he feisty? And
Just as sexy. Yes, gurl.

Nina
Thank you, gurl.

Venus
Well, as much as I would love to leave you
Two here making Enrique Cruz moments
I've got to get Ms Nina out
Those boy dregs and into some more
Intimate apparel.

Nina
Oh shit, Ms Nottage, the ball!

Venus
Lord, you so busy living looking loving like
An E. Lynn Harris book, you done forgot about
The ball. Gurl, c'mon here. Lucian's on the
Warpath. And if he finds you like this . . .

Eric
Lucian?

Nina
Right behind you, girl.
Be right back, babe.

Exit Venus and Nina.

SCENE EIGHT

Enter Deity.

Deity
Oh, 'sup man?
(*Calling off.*) Somebody order some pizza?

Eric
Oh, nah, man, I'm Eric.

Deity
You need somebody?

74

Eric

Nah, I'm just here with . . .

Deity

With?

Eric

Wilson.

Deity

Who?

Eric

Wil . . . Nina, man.

Deity

Oh. Huh.
Well, um, thank you for dropping
Her off.

Eric

He asked me to wait.

Deity

Oh did *she*?

Eric

You kinda rude to be the doorman.

Deity

Oh homie, I can show you rude, boy.

Enter the Fates.

Faith

Deity, what track is . . .

They see Eric.

Sing Halleluiah in the Sanctuary.

The Fates Three
Yes, Lord, for the rest of our days!

Deity
Pizza boy, this the Fates. Fates, this Ms Nina's
Um, friend.

Faith
Faith.

Fay
Fay.

Fate
FA TAH!

Eric
I'm Eric.

Fate
So, you here with Ms Nina?

Fay
Where is the bitch so I can congratulate her?

Eric
Are you real?

Fate
Excuse me?

Faith
Bitch, are you real?

The Fates Three
To be real!

Eric
Like real women . . . ?

Fay
Uh, uh, Ms Nina gurl, come get this one.

Eric

I'm sorry. I was just . . . I mean, how do you tell?

Fate

What, you want us to prove it to you?

Fay

Chile, today has been a time between
Lucian telling me to pull my titty out . . .

Eric

Lucian who?

Faith

Redbone gets the stare.

Deity

You know Lucian?

SCENE NINE

Enter Lucian.

Lucian

Eric! Papi, 'sup?
What you doing here, mayne?

Faith

He shakes his hand . . .

Fate

He holds an embrace . . .

The Fates Three

He . . .

Faith

Guess that answers that question.

Deity

Yeah, they know each other . . .

Deity *and* **Faith**
    Biblically.

Eric
    This is . . . You're a part of a house?

Lucian
    This is my house. To be honest, Papi,
    We're kind of busy getting ready for
    A ball.

Eric
    I know . . .

Lucian
    Oh yeah?

Eric
    I know Wilson.

    Enter Nina, without her wig, and Venus in tow.

Lucian
    Oh yeah?

Nina
    Oh hey, Lucian I was just about to get
    My . . . my bag.

    *She goes in the bag and pulls out the wig. The entire
    House, save Rey-Rey, watches as she looks at the
    Wig, then at Eric, and then puts it on.*

Faith
    The silence of the moment.

Fate
    The drizzle of rain.

Fay
    Enter Rey-Rey.

Rey-Rey
I know it's the funniest concept but when the big
Hand is on twelve and the little is creeping on eleven,
That means 'it getting late'. Y'all standing round
With your mouths agape and I have to wonder
What the . . . Ooh, hello!

Eric
Hi.

Rey-Rey
You're . . .

All (*except Eric*)
Eric!

Rey-Rey
Well damn. Don't let me be the last
To know.

Lucian
Rey-Rey, take everybody. I want to talk
To, uh, Wilson in my, um, office.

Venus
But she needs to go over . . .

Lucian
Yo no se! What the fuck! Did I
Ask you? I need to talk to you . . .
The rest of you . . . get it together.

Lucian turns to go. He passes Deity.

You got something to say, Deity? Dime' Papi . . .
Just say the word.

Lucian and Ms Nina exit.
The Fates and Rey-Rey go too.

Venus

Welcome to the House!

Eric

It's intense.

Deity

It's fucked up.

Venus

It's not all screaming and yelling, everyone
Is just a lil . . . Come with us to the ball.

Eric

Um, nah, I don't think . . .

Deity

He don't think so.

Venus

It's going to be fun.
The *only* ball . . .

Eric

Are they coming back?

Deity

Nina?

Venus

Right now she is being . . . chastised.

Deity

'Cause of you . . .

Venus

Because she walked into the light without her liner
Without her MAC factor . . .
Without her face.

Eric

Look I'm just . . . tell 'em I'm going.

Deity

Bye!

Venus

Sugar, don't leave.

Deity

Let that nigga go.

Eric

Eh man!

Venus

Don't pay him no mind. Be quiet, Adrian,
And I might let you sit next to me during
The car ride.

Eric

Is Lucian . . . are they?

Venus

Lucian belongs to no one, honey, don't be jealous.

Eric

Nah, nah, it's not like that. I met Lucian
At the club and you know we kicked it.
I didn't know he . . . ran a house.

Venus

Ran a . . . Lucian doesn't *run* a house.
He's the house father. He looks after
A house.

Deity

Huh.

Venus

Most of the time.
(*To Eric.*)You look confused.

Eric

I mean . . .

Venus

Nina likes you. I can tell. The way
Y'all were talking earlier. Like you knew
Each other for a long time. Like y'all were
Old friends.

Eric

I . . . like him too. Easy to get
Comfortable . . .

Deity

He likes to be called *she*.
You comfortable with that?

Venus

I know you not coming out your face
Talking 'bout somebody's comfort zone,
Vanessa Williams.

Eric

What's up with dude?

Venus

He hasn't been the same
Since I stopped giving him head.

Deity

I do miss it.

Venus

I give brain like I went to Yale.

Both Eric and Deity laugh until they
Notice each other laughing. They stop.

Before there was a face or Deity in
This place. Before the thrantastic three sang
Sweet melodies. There was Lucian the

Father and Rey the Mother of Light in a house
That longed for life. And one day on the steps
Of the club mansion came a little
Nina, wet and beat the fuck up. Her
Body read man, gave you butch, but secretly she
Believed she was a woman.

AN INTERLUDE

Lights up on Nina, standing near naked in
The upper room, as Mahalia would say, the wig on
Her head.

Nina

My grandmother wore a wig.
One night when I thought no one was looking I
Grabbed the wig and ran into my room and stood
Before the mirror, mirror, and snug that wig behind
My heaven-kissed ears. I couldn't believe who I saw.
It was like standing there, after a long look, to find
Someone and finally seeing who you were searching
    for . . .
Right there. Not who they told
You you were, not who they say you should be, just
Me. I couldn't walk away from the sight
So my father knocked me away from it. Guess he
Snuck in when I was sun self-bathing. Guess he might
Have been standing there all along. But he knocked me
Down. I fell into the mirror and it broke like heaven
From the first fall into a thousand pieces.

Wilson pulls the wig off.

Wilson

He called me every faggot and homo he could
Muster. And I took it. I guess I felt like I could.
Now that I knew me.

83

He saw that, though.
He took pieces of the mirror, snatched it up like a
    work tool,
And he said, he said . . .
'If you want to be a woman so bad, I'll make you
One. I made you a boy I can remake you a lil girl.'
Standing there with that piece of glass in his hand.
Gripping it so tight he cutting himself, slicing his hand,
Blood just dripping down his hand his fingers.
    I remember
Worrying about him. I wanted to grab his hand say,
'Daddy, its okay. It'll be okay. Okay?' I just stood there.
'I'll make you one,' he mumbling.
He thought he was God, I guess. Huh. I had to remind
    him that
He was barely a father.

SCENE ELEVEN

Lights shift to Lucian sitting and Nina standing.

Lucian

How you just walk in here . . .

Wilson

Lucian . . .

Lucian

B boy'd down looking like boyz to men . . .

Wilson

I know . . .

Lucian

And dragging that trade with you?

Wilson

It was raining outside I didn't want my
Make-up to get wet or my hair.

Lucian

Now you gone lie to me, Mija?

Wilson

No . . . I . . . He . . .

Lucian

Listen to me, listen, little one, I know you get lonely . . .

Wilson

I do.

Lucian

Me too. I ain't got nobody but you. You my first child
of light and I love all of you. Can your lil boy do
that?

Wilson

Maybe.

Lucian

'Maybe'? That's what you want, a maybe love?
Come here. Let me show you something, ma. Slip this on.

Wilson

Wait.

Lucian

Little one . . .

Wilson slips on the dress.

Fix . . . put your hair right.

She fixes her wig.

You see that. Now, that's my Nina. The little girl who
came
To me those years back. *Mi Nina.* See what I see . . . See?
And all that I could see, see . . .

Lucian *and* **Nina**
Was the bottom of the ocean sea, sea.

They laugh.

Lucian
My girl. We gotta get ready for the ball, lil one.
Stop fucking around, I need my lil star to shine.
You the soul of light. If ever we needed a mother . . .

Nina
Lucian!

Lucian
After Rey, after Rey, it'd be you. You know that.
Let's go get some for light.

Lights shift to Venus, Deity and Eric.

Venus
Come with us to the ball, it's gonna be the
Only good time. Mama Rey is serving some
Fashion. I'm giving you a lil face-bouquet.
And Nina . . .

Eric
Huh. Is . . . she good?

Venus
Come see. C'mon, stay.

Nina enters.

Nina
Yeah, stay.

The Fates Three enter, singing.

The Fates Three
Please honey won't you stay . . .

Eric (*laughs*)
Alright.

Enter Rey-Rey.

Rey-Rey
Do you children know the meaning of 'Let's go'?
I know it's hard. You were all brought
Up with the believing flavour flav sexy, I do sympathise.

Fates
Flava flav!

Rey-Rey
You feeling better, baby? You looked a lil
Constipated or worried earlier, you got
That all squared away?

Eric (*laughing*)
Fine, thanks.

Rey-Rey
Let me know, I keeps a Fleet enema
In my purse. A lady can never be too sure.
Let us pray.

Eric
You pray?

Rey-Rey
Honey, this is the House of Light.

Faith
The house that prays together . . .

Fay
Stays together.

Rey-Rey
Take a kneel, Eric. Venus, translate please. Just in case
God's a Lukumi after all.

Heavenly fem Father,
I am trying, desperately, to hold together

The tired and fraying edges of a house of
Children who wanna fuck everything in finger
   distance . . .

Venus
I have an addiction, okay!

Rey-Rey
I say I walked through the Valley of the Shadow of
   Death,
Fiercely.
I fear no evil.
A new day is coming . . .
And the House of Light will be bringing in the dawn
   bitch!
Bright as the morning star!

The Fates Three
Amen! Amen! Amen!

All exit, Eric trails.

SCENE TWELVE

Enter Lucian.

Lucian
My man, Eric.

Eric
Huh?

Lucian
Where you going?

Eric
To the ball.

Lucian
You ain't gone ask me?
You ain't gone say bye?

Eric

Oh, my bad man. Is it cool . . .?

Lucian

Oh, it's very cool, Papo. Very.
If that's where you wanna go?

Eric

Oh yeah.

Lucian

I mean you ain't gotta go right now.
Shit don't never start on time. E'so
FPT.

Eric

Huh?

Lucian

Faggot People Time. Always late.
You got time.
You could come inside.
We could talk in here.

Eric

Nah, I mean, I know this your house and
Everything. That you and Nina . . . that y'all . . .

Lucian

Me and Nina? Me and Nina, what?
She a kid in my house.

Eric

Right. I'm saying its cool that we kicked
It.

Lucian

You do what the fuck you please, man. Everybody else
Does.

Eric

What you saying?

Lucian
  I know you.
  You be loving and leaving niggas.

Eric
  Leaving?

Lucian
  I came to the club last night, you wasn't there.
  Dude said you had already left.

Eric
  Oh yeah. It was getting late, man. Everything
  Was 'bout to shut down.

Lucian
  You couldn't wait for me, Papi?

Eric
  No, I did, trust.

Lucian
  Had me standing there looking stupid 'n shit.

Eric
  I didn't mean to . . .

Lucian
  Then you show up to my spot with one of
  My . . . kidz.

Eric
  I wasn't trying . . . Like I said, I didn't know.
  I mean, I felt stupid waiting there all night. So . . .
  I mean, I guess we both . . .

Lucian
  Eric, it's cool, Pa. I mean, you had fun right?
  With Nina, right, you had a good time? I mean
  She got good ass, that ass is good, *verdad*?

Eric

Lucian

    Wait. Wait a minute.
    Oh shit. Eric! Eric? Ha ha!
    You let Nina fuck you. Nah,
    Hell nah, you c'mon, you let
    That fem dick get up in your back!
    That freak!
    I thought you said you like dudes . . .

Eric

    I do.

Lucian

    Like real regular masculine dudes.

Eric

    That's right.

Lucian

    Like, like Nina?
    You like trannie girls on your back, Pa?
    Nah, I know what you like, man. I got it,
    Right. I know I got it 'cause you looking
    At me like you want it, want it?

Eric

Lucian

    C'mon, Papi. Tell it to me real quick.

Eric

    They waiting.

Lucian

    Oh, you know I don't take but a minute.
    Step into my office. Real quick, real fast,
    Real nigga shit.

Eric exits into the wings. Lucian is alone on stage.

Lucian

My grandmother . . . wore a wig.
My mother . . . wore a wig. My father wore
A wig. No, not a man-wig, Not a rag to hide
His widow's peak. The nigga wore a wig. In
Secret. In a private place where he thought
No one could see. I saw.
I stumbled into him dancing around his
Bedroom for another man, dancing and prancing
Like a fucking girl, like a woman, like he was weak.
I walked into his room, I wasn't embarrassed, or scared,
I just walked right in. Curious. Not about my father.
No. Fuck 'em.
I wondered about the man my father wore a wig for.
I wondered what power he had to make my father be
A woman for him.

Lights. End of Act Two.

Act Three

Serena

Vicki . . . Dominic . . . Kate! Somebody better flicker
Them lights. Ring-a-ding-a-ling, Mother's reading!
I been standing here too long
And I been damned if I let my make-up go south like
Because intermission's too long. *Please just stop the
music, music, music.*
Uh-Uh! Get in here, Nowago!
Who put an intermission
Before a ball, any damn way! Huh? Oh, now you
shrugging,
'You don't know?'
'You don't know' do a lot shit round here.
'You don't know' left that foul stench in the men's
room. 'You don't
Know' decided the intermission to be here. When I
find 'You don't know'
I'm-a whoop 'You don't know's' ass. Turn the lights
down *low*!
Shit, now come on, give me romantical light. So I can
get this
Party started. Ow, giving pink, giving . . . I saw that!
Did you . . .
Did you . . . There is a sign that says no eating in the
theatre,
Tried to hide them snacks in your purse-pocket
backpack.
Trying to sneak some cookies from the cookie jar
when all
You need are lil Debbie's *cakes*. Sometimes in chocolate

But these the new peach cobbler. Ow! Giving Dunkin'
　　Heinz for
Your Pillsbury Doughboy!
Ooh. Look at you.
Oh yes, sir!
How much drag queen you got in you, sir?

Pause.

You want thirteen inches
More? More like seven and a half, but a nine feels
　　nicer, so I can give you an eight!
That's right. I am a drag queen, if you looking for 'the
　　real' you missed it.
Stew wrapped that ditty up a couple months back, baby.
Intermission is *ovah*! How you coming in late from
Intermission? What, you
Tried to traverse them steps? You knew you couldn't
　　catch
Them steps. You seen them steps? Bitch near 'bout fell
　　up, out,
And died on them steps. Bitch them steps give you
　　Boi George
'I'll tumble for yah. I'll tumble for yah!' Ow. Let me
　　sing if I want
To. Oh for heaven sakes, chile, let's get this show off
　　the commode!
Spot!

Loki

Serena Mother of the House of
Diabolique!

Serena

It's French, bitch! For those of you who
Don't know me, *fuck you too*!
We are here to welcome
The Legend Stars and Statements! Yes!
Welcome to the Cinderella Ball!

*'Bullet with Butterfly Wings' by Smashing Pumpkins
Blares on.*

Serena

Loki!

The music stops. Loki pops on stage.

Loki

Yes, Mama?

Serena

What I told you 'bout putting on this
Tried and sad Seattle shit?

Loki

Sorry, Mama!

Serena

Give me something with some
Stank on it. Skank on it!
Stank on yah!

A House song blares on.

Yes! Yeah, you can work a lil bit,
Don't give me much. Don't make me wait.
Give me body, yes!

All you cunty kids got a notice *today* that
We were bashing at midnight, girlies, and
You had no time, no way to prepare. I mean
We of course knew weeks ago we were going to
Throw it. But we wouldn't be evil step
Sisters and wicked stepmothers if we
Didn't do something maleficent. Aw.
It's payback in the Huxtable house tonight.
Our judges for this evening
Represent some of the most fabulous and
Legendary of bitches!

Lights dim on Serena as she speaks.
The Fates come from behind her.

Faith
It began like all balls do.

Fay
Fingers waving.

Fate
The processional of powers into the room . . .

Faith
Houses new . . .

Serena
Cream!

Fay
Old . . .

Serena
Le Beiga!

Fate
Legendary . . .

Serena
Manolo Blahnik!

Lights fade on Serena.

Fate
But soon after it began . . .

Faith
We saw the greatest of tragedies
Unfold before our eyes.

Fay
It was bloody.

Faith
Judges cursing.

The Fates Three
Chopping!

Fay
But outta darkness –

Fate
Always comes –

The Fates Three
A little Rey –

Rey-Rey, Mother of the House of Light, stands at the end of the runway. She is revealed in her FIT OUT!

Fate
Mother Light!

Faith
Classic Icon. Done up in –

The Fates Three
Pumps!

Faith
Hundred and forty-five dollars!

The Fates Three
Dress!

Fay
Balenciaga . . .

Fate
Twenty-five hundred dollars!

Faith
The Mastercard she boosted to buy all this shit . . .

The Fates Three
Priceless!

Faith
Boosting, it's everywhere you wanna be!

Fate

Shwam!

Fay

Strike !

Faith

Hold that pose!
Givin' th' kidz a lesson!

Fate

Mama who knows, *yes*!

Fay

Shwam!

Faith

Pop!

Fate

Shutting shit *down*!

Fay

Stop!

Fate

Lock!

Faith

Turn around!

The Fates Three

Give the kidz a pose!

Rey turns to do a pose. A Judge in baseball cap and hip-hop demeanour steps on to the runway. The Fates gasp.

Fay

It rarely happens that a legend gets chopped.

Faith

But when it happens –

Fate

We all feel it.

Faith

Delicate Rey.

Fay

Served like she had done back when . . .

Fate

But it wasn't enough, no . . .

The Fates Three

It wasn't enough.

*The Judge in the baseball cap sprays Rey-Rey's face
with silly string. And in the air makes a chopping sign
with his hand. Rey stands still, very still. A light on
Serena as she howls with laughter. Rey-Rey smiles,
turns and walks back out of light.*

Fay

The House of Light had just been hit hard,
Honey.

Faith

To have a legend in your house chopped, there
Was almost no recovery.

The Fates Three

Almost.

Fay

Leave it to beauty to find a way.

*Venus enters on the runway. Looking fan-fucking-
tastic!*

Fate

Venus as a boy walking androgyny!

Fay
Walking realness of face.

Fate *and* **Fay**
Walking!

Faith
Down the runaway, the runway leaving
Bitches dumbfounded.

Fay
Venus removed the hat!

Fate
To reveal more beauty.

Fay
Removed the sunglasses!

Fate
Still more beauty.

Fay
Giving the kids what they couldn't stand . . .

The Fates Three
Beauty incarnate.

Enter Loki, walking alongside Venus.

Faith
Chile some boy from the house of Di'
Abolique tried to interrupt Venus's reign
Of the category with a challenge.

Fay
Girl!

Fate
Venus was having none of that!

The Fates Three *and* **Venus**
No, ma'am!

Venus walks towards the audience alongside Loki.
They pose for the audience and the Judges.

Faith
Venus wipes her face with her hand to show
That she has . . .

Fay
Smooth natural beauty.

Faith
Loki does the same.

Fate
Smooth, natural.

Venus
Huh!

Faith
Venus goes into a pocket.

Fate
Pulls out
A handkerchief?

Fay
Bitch who carries a handkerchief?

Fate
Rubs the cloth across her face.

Venus shows the cloth.

Fay
It's clean!

Faith
She hands it to Ms Loki.

Fate
Loki rubs the cloth across his face.

Venus snatches the cloth and shows it to the Judge.

Fay
It's smeared!

With Loki-toned make-up.

Faith
Maybe she's born with it!

The Fates Three
Maybe it's Maybelline!

Fay
Yes, girl!

*Loki exits, defeated. Venus walks upstage and gives
the audience one last look before the lights burst out
on her.*

Venus
FIERCE!

Venus exits.

Fate
It was time . . .

Fay
It had ticked up on us . . .

Faith
The grand prize category.

Fay
And we needed the audience's help.

Fate
As we do now.

Faith
To bring the crowd to a frenzy is what this
Category is all about.

Fay

We were still raw with rehearsal . . .

Faith

And it didn't help that Diabolique went
First.

Fay

Bitch, the opening choreography was sick!

Loki comes in and is giving you punk rock slickness.
Reading the kids with kicks, turns and layouts.
He lip-syncs.

He pulls back a curtain to reveal darkness everlasting.
Forward from the back comes Serena giving us the
* depths*
Of Hell, kinda like Akasha, Those who must be kept,
Reading Ms Aaliyah but arisen. Honey, your mother
* needs*
A resolution! Complete with fangs, maybe.
Serena gives you legendary darkness, bi-yatch!

Lights out on Serena.

Fay

What . . .

Fate

The . . .

The Fates Three

Fuck?

Faith

I ain't neva seen a house get it together like
That.

Fay

The bitches had two weeks.

Faith
We had one night.

Faith *and* **Fay**
Get in!

Fate
It was time to pay homage to the light.

Fay
We began as man did,
With a beat . . .

Faith
We revealed character . . .

Fate
Left them breathless . . .

Fay
Gasping for more.

Faith
And there in the court of houses . . .

Fay
We crowned a new Queen Mother.

Lights cut out on the Fates Three. And up
On Nina standing downstage with a candle.
The light is royal blue. The dress she is wearing is tight.
Very fitting. She could not walk realness – Hell,
The bitch can barely walk. But she is giving
You exotic and beautiful diva!

Nina
For those who walked before.

Either in a haunting falsetto or in sync with the song
'Little Light of Mine' by the Turtle Creek Chorus Nina
Sings. The Fates can add some offstage harmony or some
Glowed face assistance if necessary.

She blows out the candle. A spot comes up on Eric.
A song modern and hot comes up.
We see the Fates
Standing behind Nina in true do-wap signature. They
Perform this song up and through the first verse and
Chorus. Giving Eric all the praise.

Enter Deity and Venus.
Bulbs flash. Lights blink on and off.
As they do a sign
That reads: 'Light!' comes on upstage. The lights
Illuminate Venus dressed in all white, looking
So sweet, and Deity in a white suit. They give us
Their best Jay Z and Beyoncé.
Deity and Venus exit.

Rey-Rey walks onto the stage. Looking stumbly and
Obviously still upset from the chopping that occurred
Earlier. She walks forward and begins posing and giving
    you old way vogue
Moves that set the kids ablaze.

The Fates Three walk up.
Launch into their song like a shark at feeding.
Huney, when I tell you these girls give you
Performance. Adding a Lil Jay set. Ms Choreography,
Let's do it up, hello!
At the end they stop lip-syncing.
While they do
This enters Lucian.

Lucian

Introducing the new Mother of the House of Light.
Miss Venus of Light.

Venus walks in looking stunning. I don't
Even know how to describe the bitch. So costume,
Do your best, girl! Lucian hands Venus a crown.
The entire house, save Rey-Rey, stands in

That tableau we saw earlier as the Fates finish
Their Amens in perfect harmony and volume.

The Fates Three
Amen! Ahhhhhmen!

Venus
Somebody get the lights.

Lights out on everyone on stage. A soft spot on Rey-Rey in the upper room.

Act Four

Fate in a soft light sings a sad song.

SCENE ONE

Nina
You loved it!

Eric
I don't know about all that . . .

Venus
Look at your face, you can't hide nothing,
Light skin. Your face, it's all over your face.

Eric
I . . .

Nina *and* **Venus**
He loved it.

Faith
Especially when we got to the grand march out.

Fay
Yes, bitch!

Faith
That was something serious.

Fay
For once there was no fighting at the end.

Venus
Wasn't nothing to fight about. We worked.

Eric

It was hot.

Fay

My God, Venus, you looked so beautiful.

Faith

My face was on the floor when Lucian made you . . .

Fay *and* **Faith**

MOTHER LIGHT!

Venus

YOU? Bitch, you talking 'bout somebody losing it?
And this bitch in the back talking 'bout some
'Don't you die on me, Shelby!'

Nina

Fight, Shelby!

Venus

What do I do to deserve a sister like you?

Nina

It's only because I know you are the . . . perfect
Mother.

Venus

Good girl, I thought you'd be lil jelly.

Nina

I am. I just decided to give it to, give it to Mama.

Venus

Yes. So if you want to . . .

Nina *and* **Venus**

You got the GREEN LIGHT.

Enter Deity.

Deity

You look like the morning star, baby.

Venus

Thank you, Deity.

Eric

Why they call you Deity?

Venus

He is the God of the DJs.

Eric

They should call you something like Apollo, right?
Venus and Apollo?

Deity

What the fuck they call you?

Venus

Deity!

Deity

Gemini? Fake-ass nigga!

Nina

What are you talking about?

Venus

Hey, cut out the arguing now.

Deity

Nina, let me talk to you . . .

Nina

What? Hold on, stop pulling my arm, boy.
What's wrong with you.

Deity

You need to . . .

Fate hums.

Nina

Wait a minute! I be right back, angel.

Fay

Who the hell is playing . . .

Faith

That depressing ass song!

Venus

It's coming from upstairs.

Exit Faith, Fay and Venus. Lights fade on Fate. Nina and Deity stand opposite Eric.

SCENE TWO

Nina

What, man?

Deity

Wilson, this kid is playing you?

Nina

Yessir, and I like the game he plays.

Deity

C'mon, Wil, stop playing.

Nina

Why you keep calling me that?

Deity

That's your name.

Nina

Nina.

Deity

Nina, he slept with Lucian.

Nina

I know that. You think I don't know that?
Who hasn't slept with Lucian? They knew

Each other before. What am I supposed to
Do?

Deity
No . . .

Nina
No what?

Deity
They were fucking around before the ball.
Tonight. Probably during the ball.

Nina
Oh.

Deity
You know Lucian. That's what he does.
He messes around with some young
Kat and then the next minute he asking them . . .

Nina
To be in his house.

Deity
I just wanted to tell you.

Nina
You told me.

Deity
Listen, let's . . .

Nina
Hold on.

SCENE THREE

Nina (*to Eric*)
Angel . . .

Enter Lucian.

Lucian

That's a good name for him.

Eric

Lucian . . .

Lucian

Angel. Anjel. You be the first Angel
Of Light. You like that, Papo? You want
To be in the light?

Eric

I don't know . . . I mean, I don't do drag.

Lucian

Neither do I. I look like some punk fag
Walking drag. Nah. I'm a man. We need
Some more men round here. Right, Deity?

Deity

Fuck you.

Enter Venus.

Venus

Deity! I need you.

Deity

Baby, what's wrong?

Venus

She locked the door. The music's loud
But I can hear her, sound like she sick.

Eric

Who?

Lucian

Rey-Rey.

Venus

I need you to come break open the
Door.

Deity

Call an ambulance.

Venus

I already told Faith. C'mon.

Lucian

Wait. Don't let her call.

Deity

Wait! For what?

Venus

Rey-Rey is . . .

Lucian

Break the door down like she said.

Deity

WHAT!

Lucian

Open the door see how bad
. . . I'll stop the girl from calling.
Go!

Lucian, Deity and Venus exit.

SCENE FOUR

Eric

What's going on?

Wilson

I never seem to know.

Eric

You not gone go see?

Wilson

Venus is the mother now, she can handle it.

Eric

You talking like . . . like Wilson.

Wilson

I met you as Wilson, I should
Say goodbye the same way.

Eric

Goodbye? Where you going?

Wilson

Nowhere. Ain't got nowhere else to go.

Eric

You asking me to leave?

Wilson

Before he comes back.

Eric

Is this about . . . with Lucian?

Wilson

No. This about us.

Eric

Ey, man, I like you a lot.

Wilson

I know.

Eric

This whole scene, it's . . . it's . . .
I mean, don't you get confused?

Wilson

No, I don't.

Eric

Oh. I guess that's how you know you belong
Or not.

Wilson

Yes.

Eric
I had a real good time today.

Wilson
When? With me?

Eric
You're the only good time I've had.

Wilson puts the wig back on.

Will you tell everybody I said bye?

Nina
They won't even know you missing.

Eric
Damn, that's vicious.

Nina
You don't know the half.

Eric
Will you know?
Will you know I'm missing?

Nina
I always have.

Eric
Night, Nina, goodnight.

Exit Eric.

SCENE FIVE

Faith
Deity stumbles in.

Fay
Holding his face.

Venus

No! Deity, I know. Let it go.

Lucian

Let him go. Let him come to
Daddy.

Deity

I got your daddy.

Nina

What's going on?

Deity

This motherfucker's crazy!

Nina

What's wrong?

Venus

Rey-Rey swallowed some pills. A lot, we
Think.

Nina

Call the . . .

Deity

That's what I said. Lucian's got his finger
Down her throat, holding her head over the
Toilet. I know you got that throat inspection
Game on lock, but you ain't a fucking doctor.

Lucian

Look at you, Deity, so upset. I'm crazy?

Deity

Lost your fucking tree, monkey.

Lucian

Like you lost your house, Adrian.

Venus

What?

Lucian
And so you know, the next time you
Might wanna think twice before you
Drive in the ER with a Mija face full
Of drag and stomach full of pills. You
See how long she'll stay in the hospital.
See how long she stay in for observation.
It's near 'bout morning, man,
Don't you think you should be getting
Home? Mama? See that your . . . friend gets
Home safe.

Exit Lucian.

Nina
Is she okay?

Venus
Yeah.

Faith
She's talking now.

Venus
He knew what to do.

Deity
This time.

Venus
Adrian.

Deity
Come on, this . . .

Venus
I hear you.

Deity
We can leave . . .

Venus
No!

Deity

We can start our own . . .

Venus

Listen to me!

Deity

We can . . .

Venus

I need you to be quiet, okay? I'm not going anywhere,
Boi. These are . . . my best friends and
My only family: here. I am the Mother
Of this House, I can't just walk out.
You go 'head. Go 'head, Papi. This wasn't never for you.

Deity

What about you? You, for me?

Venus

You know where to find me
When you need me.

Deity

You my baby?

Faith

She rolls her eyes.

Venus

Yes.

Deity

You *the* baby?

Fay

Through clenched teeth.

Venus

Yes. I'm the baby. Now get away
From me before I spit up on you.

Deity

Nina. Ladies . . .
My baby.

Fay

Exit Deity.

Faith

They shoot her a look.

Fay

I mean Adrian, with so much swagger.

SCENE SIX

Nina

Well, come along, *baby*, it's getting late.

Venus

Oh no, ma'am, baby to him,
In the House of Light I am
Mother Venus.

They laugh. Enter Rey-Rey, held up by Fate.

Rey-Rey

Never thought I would see one of my
Babies become a Mother.

Venus

You'll always be Mama.

Nina

And when she has kids. you'll be a . . .

Rey-Rey

You let that G word come out your mouth,
Nina, and chile . . .

Nina

We need to think of a new
Name.

Venus

Like Mother Superior . . .

Nina

Or the Top Mother!

Rey-Rey

Oh no, honey, I am not on top o'
Nothing. Thank you, Fate.
Yes, ma'am, how they say,
I like my meat down low and my
Top jet black.

Venus

Listen at you!

Nina

Misquoting Ms TI!

Venus

You'll be back on the runway giving
Legendary up in Timberlands soon.

Rey-Rey

Well, like the south I shall rise again.

Fate

Hold it!

Fay

Where did sweet thang go?

Nina

Huh. Too much sugar and not enough
Nutrients.

Rey-Rey

That's okay, girl. I understand. I had a

Sweet tooth too once. It's been giving
Me cavities ever since.

Rey-Rey held up by Nina and Venus exit.

Fay
My man's gone now.

Faith
Hey, get your singing self over here.

Fate
The shows over, Synergy.

Fay
Sorry, Faith.

Faith
Its alright, Fay.

Fate and Fay exit.

A little light for Eric the Red.

Eric
My grandmother wore a wig . . .

Lights.